Shakespeare on the Double!™

Twelfth Night

translated by

Mary Ellen Snodgrass

WILEY
Wiley Publishing, Inc.

Published by Wiley Publishing, Inc., Hoboken, New Jersey

Library of Congress Cataloging-in-Publication data is available from the publisher upon request.

ISBN: 978-0-470-21277-6

Printed in the United States of America

10 9 8 7 6 5 4 3 2 1

Book design by Melissa Auciello-Brogan
Book production by Wiley Publishing, Inc. Composition Services

Contents

About the Translator

Mary Ellen Snodgrass is an award-winning author of textbooks and general reference works and a former columnist for the *Charlotte Observer*. A member of Phi Beta Kappa, she graduated magna cum laude from the University of North Carolina at Greensboro and Appalachian State University and holds degrees in English, Latin, psychology, and education of gifted children.

Acknowledgment

Thanks to Dr. Suzanne Kramer Jeffers of Lenoir-Rhyne College for her advice on interpretation.

Introduction

Shakespeare on the Double! Twelfth Night provides the full text of the Bard's play side by side with an easy-to-read modern English translation that you can understand. You no longer have to wonder what exactly "like a worm i' the bud" means! You can read the Shakespearean text on the left-hand pages and check the right-hand pages when Shakespeare's language stumps you. Or you can read only the translation, which enables you to understand the action and characters without struggling through the Shakespearean English. You can even read both, referring back and forth easily between the original text and the modern translation. Any way you choose, you can now fully understand every line of the Bard's masterpiece!

We've also provided you with some additional resources:

- **Brief synopsis** of the plot and action offers a broad-strokes overview of the play.
- **Comprehensive character list** covers the actions, motivations, and characteristics of each major player.
- **Visual character map** displays who the major characters are and how they relate to one another.
- **Cycle of love** pinpoints the sequence of love in the play, including who *truly* loves whom, and who *mistakenly* loves whom.
- **Reflective questions** help you delve even more into the themes and meanings of the play.

Reading Shakespeare can be slow and difficult. No more! With *Shakespeare on the Double! Twelfth Night,* you can read the play in language that you can grasp quickly and thoroughly.

Synopsis

ACT I

Scene 1

At Illyria, a country east of Italy, Duke Orsino enjoys romantic music that echoes his infatuation for the Countess Olivia. His servant Valentine returns from Maria, the Countess Olivia's chambermaid, to report that Olivia has rejected Orsino's love message. In grief for the death of her brother, who has served as guardian since their father died, Olivia pledges to remain veiled and secluded for seven years. Orsino wishes that she could promise that same dedication to him. He withdraws to a bower to enjoy the pose of the wounded lover.

Scene 2

Viola, a passenger on the captain's ship on the Adriatic Sea, escapes drowning. The captain believes that Viola's twin brother Sebastian rescued himself from the wreckage by lashing his body to a floating mast. Viola rewards her rescuer with gold coins. She learns from the captain about Duke Orsino, an old bachelor friend of her deceased father, and of Orsino's courtship of the Countess Olivia. With the captain's aid, Viola abandons women's clothes, disguises herself as a eunuch, and seeks a position in Orsino's household.

Scene 3

Sir Toby Belch, Olivia's uncle, is uncomfortable living with a niece who doesn't share his exuberant joy in life. Maria, Olivia's chambermaid, scolds Sir Toby for late-night carousing with Sir Andrew Aguecheek, whom Toby brought to Illyria to court the Countess. Toby excuses his drinking as toasts to his niece's health. Maria exchanges witty put-downs with Sir Andrew, a self-important dilettante.

In despair that the Countess Olivia rejects him, Sir Andrew threatens to return home. Sir Toby depends on Sir Andrew to pay for their drunken binges. Sir Toby convinces his guest to continue courting Olivia, who spurns Duke Orsino. Sir Andrew promises to stay another month.

Scene 4

In private, Valentine chats with Viola, a household servant disguised as Cesario. Valentine informs Cesario that the Duke is fond of his new staff member, who entered service three days earlier. Orsino sends Cesario to convince Olivia to accept Orsino's marriage proposal. Cesario doubts that Olivia will see him; Orsino believes that so sweet a boy cannot fail. The Duke urges his messenger to take four or five servants with him and to stay until he succeeds. If Cesario succeeds, Orsino promises to reward his messenger handsomely. Viola regrets that she must persuade Olivia to wed the man whom Viola herself loves.

Scene 5

Maria warns the jester Feste of the danger of leaving Countess Olivia's residence without permission. Feste makes light of threatened punishments. Olivia scolds Feste, who alters her angry mood by proving she is foolish to grieve for a brother who is in heaven. Malvolio, Olivia's steward, adds his condemnation of Feste's waywardness. Olivia, who is aware of Malvolio's pompous disdain for others, silences Malvolio by accusing him of egotism.

Maria announces Cesario's arrival with a message from the Duke. Sir Toby is already too drunk to help Olivia refuse unwelcome company. Malvolio tries to turn Cesario away, but the boy declines to leave without carrying out his mission. To Olivia's questions, Malvolio describes the messenger as a handsome youth.

When Olivia meets Cesario, she wears a veil and refuses to identify herself. Maria tries to eject the impudent boy. His elegant love message from Orsino wins Olivia's affection. Olivia again rejects the Duke's marriage proposal, but she rewards Cesario with coins, which he declines. She encourages another visit from the messenger, whom she loves. To assure Cesario's return, Olivia dispatches Malvolio with a ring that she claims to refuse. The ruse reveals her love for Cesario.

ACT II

Scene 1

Engulfed in despair, Sebastian mourns the death of Viola, whom he assumes drowned in the shipwreck. They are the orphaned twins of Sebastian of Messaline. Antonio, Sebastian's rescuer, becomes the outsider's companion. Moved to tears, Sebastian proposes to leave Antonio behind rather than spread his ill fortune to Antonio. After Sebastian departs to meet Duke Orsino, Antonio resolves to pursue Sebastian, even though Antonio risks danger at Orsino's residence.

Scene 2

Malvolio pursues Cesario through the streets and returns the ring from Olivia. When Cesario shows reluctance to accept it, Malvolio tosses the ring on the ground. Viola interprets the ring as evidence that Olivia loves Cesario. The messenger correctly surmises that the ring is a ruse to draw Cesario back to Olivia's home. Viola regrets how easily men deceive impressionable women. The entanglement of attractions—Viola for Orsino, Orsino for Olivia, Olivia for Cesario/Viola—proves too complicated for Viola. She hopes that time will work out the details.

Scene 3

After midnight, Feste, Sir Andrew, and Sir Toby enjoy wine at Olivia's residence. Feste entertains with a love song. Maria warns them that their singing is too noisy. Malvolio adds his disapproval of carousing at the Countess's home and implies that Olivia would like Sir Toby to live elsewhere. Sir Toby annoys Malvolio, who promises to inform the Countess of her uncle's impertinence.

Maria wearies of Malvolio's officiousness. She plots to ridicule his pretensions by courting him in anonymous letters written in a handwriting similar to Olivia's. Maria hopes that Malvolio will believe that the letters are intended for him. Her cunning and spunk impress Sir Toby. He tries to encourage Sir Andrew into remaining at the residence to pay for their nightly revelry.

Scene 4

When Viola returns to the Duke in the morning, Orsino calls for an old-fashioned love song. With Cesario, the Duke discusses his affection for Olivia. Cesario hints at loving an older sweetheart who looks like Orsino. Orsino counsels the youth to court younger women.

To assuage the Duke's melancholy, Feste sings of unrequited love. Orsino pays Feste for the song. The Duke declares himself a more persistent lover than any woman could be. Cesario implies that her sister suffered from a secret and unrequited love. Cesario departs on another trek to the Countess with a renewed pledge of love from the Duke.

Scene 5

Maria leaves an anonymous love letter on the garden path for Malvolio to find. She urges Fabian, Sir Andrew, and Sir Toby to hide in the boxwood hedge to laugh at the steward's egotistical posturing. Malvolio believes that Maria is fond of him. He fantasizes himself as contentedly wed to Olivia for three months. He intends to use his power as the Countess's husband to command staff members and to demoralize Sir Toby for merry-making. The upstart enrages Toby.

Malvolio locates the anonymous letter and recognizes the handwriting. He decides to do anything the Countess wants to win her love. He promises to smile at Olivia. He deliberately dresses in yellow hose and ties his garters around his knee in a bow. Sir Toby wants to marry Maria for thinking up the clever deception. Maria and her coconspirators gleefully celebrate the success of the deception.

ACT III

Scene 1

On return to the Countess's garden, Cesario enjoys a humorous tit-for-tat with Feste. Without mentioning her disguise, she reveals that she is in love with a man. She comments that Feste makes his living by being witty. After Sir Andrew and Sir Toby admit Cesario to the Countess's garden, Sir Andrew intends to imitate Cesario's skill with words.

Olivia refuses to hear anything more about the Duke. She reveals her infatuation with Cesario and apologizes for sending the spurious ring as a trick to lure him back to her residence. In pity for the Countess, the messenger gives no encouragement to their impossible relationship. Olivia sinks into despair and invites Cesario to return.

Scene 2

Eavesdropping from the orchard, Sir Andrew witnesses Olivia's affection for Cesario. Sir Andrew doubts his suit can succeed. Fabian and Sir Toby assure him that Olivia is aware of Sir Andrew's presence and they bait him to make him jealous. Sir Toby believes that Sir Andrew has missed an opportunity to impress the Countess.

Sir Toby goads Sir Andrew into writing a formal challenge to a duel against Cesario. Sir Andrew departs to compose a belligerent letter. Fabian compliments Sir Toby for manipulating Sir Andrew like a puppet. Fabian and Sir Toby anticipate that the cowardly Sir Andrew and the boy Cesario will avoid combat. Maria reports that Malvolio is wearing yellow hose and garters tied at the knee for his service to Olivia. The conspirators look forward to some fun.

Scene 3

Sebastian is grateful that Antonio follows him about Illyria. Antonio intends to protect Sebastian in unfamiliar territory. Antonio urges Sebastian to lodge that evening at the Elephant and intends to order their dinner. Because Duke Orsino's men consider Antonio an enemy, the sea captain must stay off the streets while Sebastian sightsees. Antonio offers Sebastian his wallet for the purchase of trinkets and promises to meet Sebastian an hour later.

Scene 4

Maria warns the Countess Olivia that Malvolio seems bewitched. The steward bemuses his mistress by appearing in yellow hose and garters tied at the knee and by smiling at her. The Countess believes Malvolio's bizarre behavior is midsummer madness. When Cesario seeks an audience, Olivia urges Maria to ask Sir Toby to tend to Malvolio, whose service the Countess values. Fabian and Sir Toby imply that a demon possesses Malvolio. The standard treatment is to lock the victim in a dark room. Sir Toby compliments Sir Andrew on the gutless letter challenging Cesario to a duel without actually slandering the victim. Sir Toby intends to deliver a verbal challenge that will terrify Cesario.

When Olivia faces Cesario, she courts him passionately and gives him a brooch containing her picture. Cesario remains loyal to his master. Sir Toby challenges Cesario to face a fierce, vigorous swordsman who has already killed three men. Cesario quails at the thought of dueling an expert in Olivia's orchard. Sir Toby informs Sir Andrew that Cesario is a fearless opponent who taught fencing to the ruler of Persia. Sir Andrew offers his horse Capilet as a bribe to call off the duel.

To Cesario, Sir Toby declares that Sir Andrew must carry out the duel as a matter of honor. Cesario confides to herself that a wound would betray her disguise. Antonio appears and brandishes his sword to defend the twin he assumes is Sebastian. Two officers arrest Antonio for past crimes. Before departing to jail, Antonio asks Sebastian for cash. Cesario declares to know nothing about Antonio or his wallet, but offers half of her pocket money.

As the officers haul Antonio to jail, he accuses Viola of ingratitude. Because Antonio refers to her as Sebastian, she concludes that her brother must have survived the shipwreck. After her departure, Fabian and Sir Toby declare Cesario a cowardly rabbit. Sir Andrew renews his verbal challenge.

ACT IV

Scene 1

On a street before Countess Olivia's house, Feste encounters Sebastian, who knows nothing of Cesario. Sebastian gives Feste a coin and threatens the joker if he doesn't stop pestering him. Sir Andrew slaps Sebastian as though he were Cesario. To Sir Andrew's attack, Sebastian trounces him. Feste hurries to report the squabble to the Countess. Meanwhile, Sir Toby threatens Sebastian with a sword.

On arrival at the street, Olivia banishes Sir Toby for his persistently uncivil behavior. She speaks in private to Sebastian about her uncle's drunken pranks. She regrets the violence against Sebastian and woos him as though he were Cesario. Sebastian thinks he is dreaming, but he accepts her advances.

Scene 2

Maria and her fellow plotters send a priest to console Malvolio in the dark room in the Countess's house. Feste, dressed in the habit and fake beard of Sir Topas, impresses Sir Toby with his acting. Feste refutes Malvolio's complaint about the unlighted cell and refuses to help Malvolio until he concurs with Pythagoras's belief in reincarnation. Already in serious trouble with his niece, Sir Toby enjoys the trick, but wants to end the extended harassment of Malvolio.

Feste returns to the dark room, where Malvolio pleads for a candle, pen, ink, and paper to compose a note to Olivia entreating her rescue. In the dark, Feste plays two parts, that of Sir Topas and of himself. Malvolio promises to reward Feste well for alerting the Countess to her steward's predicament. Feste goes out to fetch a candle, paper, pen, and ink.

Scene 3

Sebastian ponders his good fortune in meeting Olivia and in instantly winning her love. He admires the pearl she gave him. He needs Antonio's advice and wonders why his friend did not keep their appointment at the Elephant. Olivia summons a priest to a private chapel to conduct a marriage. She intends to keep their union a secret until they choose to hold a public celebration. Sebastian vows to be loyal to her.

ACT V

Scene 1

Duke Orsino, accompanied by Cesario, arrives at the street in front of Olivia's house and recognizes members of her staff. The officers return with Antonio. The angry privateer lambastes Sebastian as a disloyal friend who has lived with Antonio for three months. Orsino recognizes the man as a pirate who attacked his ships *Phoenix* and *Tiger* near Crete. The Duke defends his servant from Antonio's accusations.

At Olivia's renewed rejection of his suit, Orsino is outraged to detect her affection for Cesario. The Duke threatens to kill his beloved servant boy. Viola offers to die for the master whom she loves. Olivia refers to Cesario as "husband" and interprets his duplicity as fear of the Duke. To the confused gathering, Olivia calls the priest, who declares that he joined Cesario in wedlock to Olivia two hours earlier. The Duke banishes Cesario.

Sir Toby limps in, and Sir Andrew complains of head wounds inflicted by Cesario. Dr. Dick is too drunk to bandage them. When Sebastian appears and apologizes for striking Olivia's uncle, the mysterious accusations begin to make sense. Sebastian reunites with Antonio; Viola recognizes her brother. Orsino pledges his love to Viola. She explains that Malvolio has jailed the captain who keeps her female clothing.

Olivia summons Malvolio from his dark cell to free the captain. Feste presents Malvolio's letter to the Countess. Meanwhile, the Duke promises marriage to Viola. Malvolio confronts Olivia with the love letter. Olivia identifies the handwriting as Maria's and promises to let Malvolio punish his tormenters. Fabian intercedes for Maria and explains that Malvolio deserved trickery for his discourtesy. Fabian announces Sir Toby's marriage to Maria. Because Malvolio stalks out vowing to get even with the plotters, Olivia regrets her steward's humiliation. The Duke promises to host a celebration of a double wedding to the twins. Feste concludes the play with a song about human suffering.

List of Characters

ORSINO The Duke of Illyria, also called Count Orsino, indulges himself in romantic fantasy and melodramatic lovesickness. He caroms from courtship of the Countess Olivia and complaint at being rejected, to infatuation with Viola, who is disguised as the page Cesario. A satiric figure for inconsistency, self-delusion, and exhibitionism, Orsino enjoys the pose of the frustrated, melancholy lover and offers half-hearted compassion for Malvolio after the steward wanders offstage vowing vengeance on his tormentors. Jolting Orsino to reality is Viola's admission that she is female.

VIOLA/CESARIO The twin sister of Sebastian, Viola, an aristocrat from Messaline, gains admiration for her wit, devotion, passion, and pluck. After her loss of Sebastian in a lethal shipwreck in the Adriatic Sea, she assumes herself brotherless and unguarded in Illyria. In the disguise of Cesario, she protects herself from harm. Meanwhile, she develops love for Duke Orsino, whom she must serve as page and go-between with the Countess Olivia. Complications arise from the messages Viola/Cesario delivers from the Duke to the Countess Olivia, who falls in love with Viola's male persona. As Cesario, Viola proves persistent and committed to her master, but admits that the three-way love entanglement is beyond her ability to resolve.

SEBASTIAN The twin of Viola, Sebastian expresses grief for his lost sister and gratitude to Antonio, a buddy who introduces Sebastian to Illyria. Unaware that his twin is near disguised as the male Cesario, Sebastian is baffled by mistaken identity. To satisfy the Countess Olivia's passion for Viola/Cesario, Sebastian accepts Olivia and fights off opposition by her uncle, Sir Toby Belch, and by the foppish Sir Andrew Aguecheek. Sebastian's aggressions against Sir Andrew establish for the audience the difference between behaviors and expectations for the male and female twins of Sebastian of Messaline.

ANTONIO A sea captain, Antonio accompanies Sebastian after rescuing him from shipwreck off Illyria. At Duke Orsino's court, Antonio produces comic confusion by spotting Viola disguised as Cesario and believing him to be Sebastian. The Duke's threat to kill Antonio heightens an ominous atmosphere in an unknown realm, where the seaman must cower in an inn to avoid retribution for past wrongs. At the eruption of violence, Antonio manifests his friendship for Sebastian by protecting Cesario, Sebastian's double, from a duel. Antonio's confusion releases anguish in Viola, who realizes that her twin survived the shipwreck.

CAPTAIN A seaman and rescuer of Viola, the Captain represents optimism in his belief that the twins will reunite. A courteous, refined man, he leads the way to Duke Orsino's court and helps Viola disguise herself for service with Illyrian nobility.

VALENTINE A gentleman attending Duke Orsino, Valentine carries love notes from the Duke to the Countess Olivia. His emblematic name suggests the flowery, insincere content of courtship messages delivered first to Olivia, then to Cesario.

CURIO A gentleman attending Duke Orsino, Curio is a virtually faceless hangon at court whose main job is placating his superior.

SIR TOBY BELCH The Countess Olivia's parasitic uncle, Sir Toby Belch is modeled on the ingratiating houseguests of Greek and Roman comedy. Rowdy to the extreme, he indulges in drinking, joking, and merrymaking. As part of his role as a knight, he is accomplished at bar-room songs, dancing, and the dueling code. A foil for the sour, overly fastidious Malvolio, Sir Toby mentors Sir Andrew Aguecheek in carousing and courting Olivia while fleecing him of cash for nightly debauchery. Sir Toby's self-indulgence precipitates a cruel joke on Malvolio and a duel that could cost the lives of Sebastian, Cesario, and Sir Andrew. Because of the success of Malvolio's humiliation, Sir Toby offers to marry Maria, the clever originator of the plot. The alliance suggests a suitable mating on a par with the Sebastian/Olivia and Orsino/Viola betrothals.

SIR ANDREW AGUECHEEK Aging squire at the home of the Countess Olivia, Sir Andrew Aguecheek stretches out his visit in Illyria to gain Olivia's love. Rich and foolish, he becomes the dupe of her uncle, Sir Toby Belch, who exploits their friendship by cadging funds to pay bar tabs. Sir Andrew plays the fool in his self-delusion that he is a witty lothario and a fighter capable of dueling against Cesario, a younger, more agile opponent. After Maria plots a ruse to humiliate Malvolio, Sir Andrew drops his pursuit of Olivia and proposes marriage to the chambermaid.

MALVOLIO The Countess Olivia's preening, pompous steward, Malvolio is a comic villain who meets his comeuppance in the secondary plot. After Sir Toby Belch and Maria conspire to humiliate the humorless steward, he reveals an urge to rise in station through fastidious behavior and appropriate dress. The duality of Malvolio lies in his hypocritical fawning on his mistress and his rudeness to Feste and Cesario. Fantasizing a rise in status as Olivia's husband, he provides the audience with a model of the unrepentent self-promoter. Despite his vanity and duplicity, he has reason to complain of misdiagnosis as a lunatic and confinement in a dark room.

FABIAN The Countess Olivia's servant and possible distant relative, Fabian befriends Sir Toby Belch and helps him convince Sir Andrew Aguecheek to prolong his suit for Olivia. As a friend of Maria, Fabian abets the plot to ridicule Malvolio. Unlike the stodgy steward, Fabian prefers reconciliation to revenge. He promotes the duel between Sir Andrew and Cesario and hopes that the resolution ends without rancor.

FESTE/SIR TOPAS The Countess Olivia's truant jester, Feste is the wise fool who spends time at the court of Duke Orsino in hopes of coins for his japes. Feste tends the drunken Sir Toby Belch and sings about the brevity of life and young love. As an antidote to the ill will of the steward Malvolio, Feste spreads cheer. He teases Malvolio during immurement in the dark room by posing as the curate Sir Topas, a parody of the pious Puritan clergy. Through cajolery, Feste lifts Olivia's funereal spirit at the death of her brother and chips away at Duke Orsino's posturing over unrequited love for Olivia.

COUNTESS OLIVIA A wealthy noblewoman and estate owner, the Countess Olivia is recently bereaved of father and brother. She mirrors her suitor Orsino's emoting by retreating into seclusion to mourn her brother. A well-rounded character, she is uninterested in Orsino's courtship, but she is capable of enjoying Feste's teasing and of worrying about Malvolio's sudden and inexplicably odd dress and flighty behavior. She commiserates over his enemies' trickery. In irrational excess, she woos Cesario and impetuously summons a priest to unite her with Sebastian, Cesario's twin.

MARIA The Countess Olivia's chambermaid, Maria is the clever servant who oversees the coming and going of visitors. She is angry enough at the grumpy steward Malvolio to plot his downfall. Contributing to her connivance is the ability to forge a love letter in Olivia's handwriting. The playwright forgives Maria and requites her long infatuation with Sir Toby Belch, a suitable husband who balances her rationality and good nature with a bubbly good humor.

Character Map

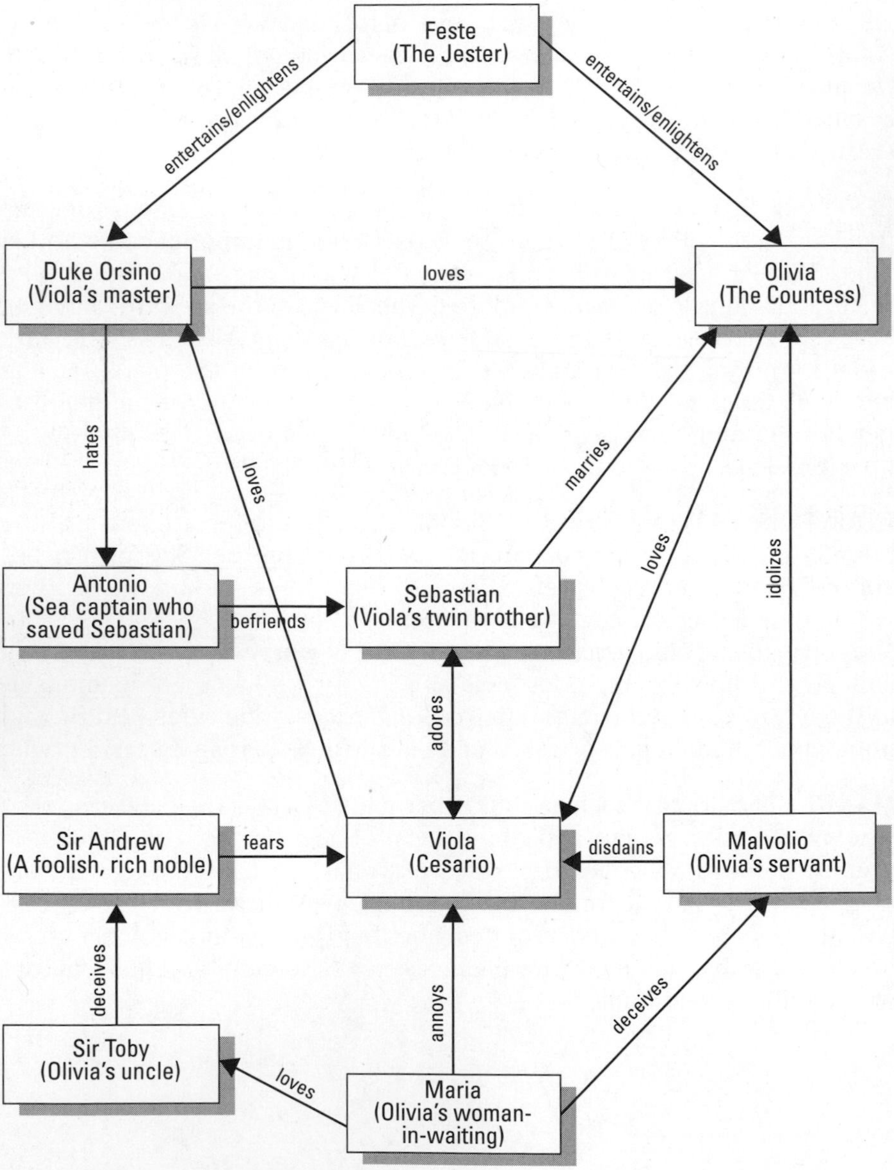

Cycle of Love

A shipwreck separates a sister and brother. The following graphic outlines the sister's search for her sibling and clarifies entanglements preceding her marriage to the lover of her choice.

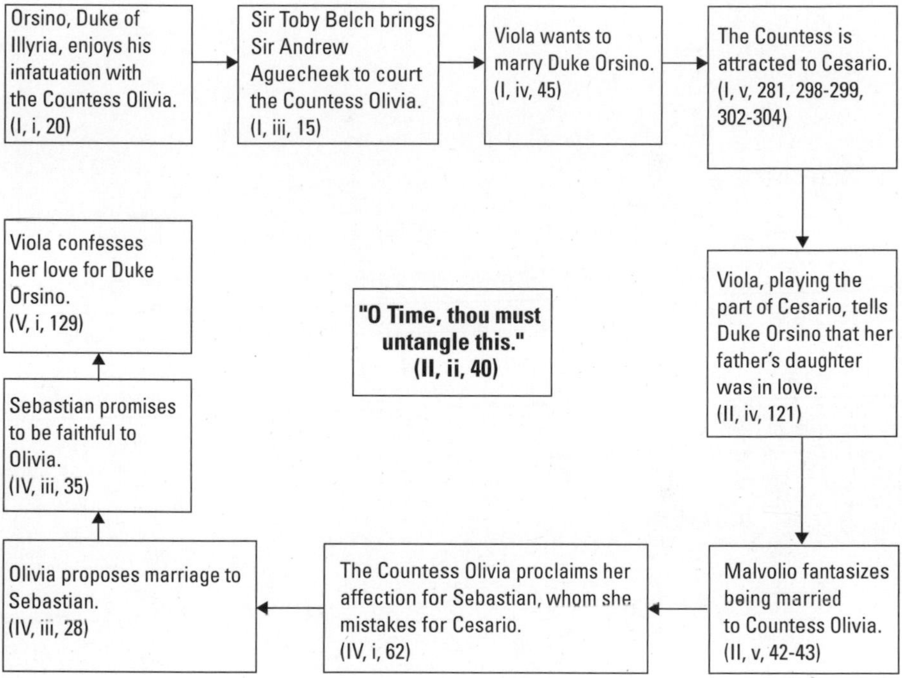

Orsino, Duke of Illyria, enjoys his infatuation with the Countess Olivia. (I, i, 20)
Sir Toby Belch brings Sir Andrew Aguecheek to court the Countess Olivia. (I, iii, 15)
Viola wants to marry Duke Orsino. (I, iv, 45)
The Countess is attracted to Cesario. (I, v, 281, 298-299, 302-304)
Viola, playing the part of Cesario, tells Duke Orsino that her father's daughter was in love. (II, iv, 121)
Malvolio fantasizes being married to Countess Olivia. (II, v, 42-43)
The Countess Olivia proclaims her affection for Sebastian, whom she mistakes for Cesario. (IV, i, 62)
Olivia proposes marriage to Sebastian. (IV, iii, 28)
Sebastian promises to be faithful to Olivia. (IV, iii, 35)
Viola confesses her love for Duke Orsino. (V, i, 129)
"O Time, thou must untangle this." (II, ii, 40)

Shakespeare's
Twelfth Night

ACT I, SCENE 1

A room in the Duke's palace.

[Enter DUKE, CURIO, and other Lords; Musicians attending]

DUKE
If music be the food of love, play on;
Give me excess of it, that, surfeiting,
The appetite may sicken, and so die.
That strain again! it had a dying fall.
O, it came o'er my ear like the sweet south
That breathes upon a bank of violets,
Stealing and giving odour! Enough; no more.
'Tis not so sweet now as it was before.
O spirit of love! how quick and fresh art thou!
That, nothwithstanding thy capacity
Receiveth as the sea, nought enters there,
Of what validity and pitch soe'er,
But falls into abatement and low price,
Even in a minute: so full of shapes is fancy,
That it alone is high fantastical.

CURIO
Will you go hunt, my lord?

DUKE
What, Curio?

CURIO
The hart.

DUKE
Why, so I do, the noblest that I have.
O, when mine eyes did see Olivia first,
Methought she purged the air of pestilence!
That instant was I turn'd into a hart;
And my desires, like fell and cruel hounds,
E'er since pursue me.
[Enter VALENTINE]
How now! what news from her?

VALENTINE
So please my lord, I might not be admitted;
But from her handmaid do return this answer:
The element itself, till seven years' heat,
Shall not behold her face at ample view;
But, like a cloistress, she will veiled walk
And water once a day her chamber round
With eye-offending brine: all this to season
A brother's dead love, which she would keep fresh
And lasting in her sad remembrance.

ACT I, SCENE 1

A room in the palace of Duke Orsino in Illyria east of Italy.

[DUKE ORSINO, his servant CURIO, and other lords enter with musicians entertaining them.]

DUKE If love feeds on music, play more music. Play excessive tunes that will fill me up and overfeed and kill my desire. That melody again! Its rhythm sounds like dying. The sound swept over my ear like a southern breeze spreading the fragrance of a bed of violets. Stop. Play no more music. It sounds less sweet this time. Oh, love, you have a lively, fresh spirit. Whatever the circumstance, love is as bottomless as the sea. Whatever the value or angle, nothing enters love without losing power and price within seconds. Imagination is so filled with visions that it is capable of endless fantasies.

CURIO Are you going hunting, my lord?

DUKE Hunting what, Curio?

CURIO Deer.

DUKE I'm hunting the grandest heart I've ever pursued. When I first saw the Countess Olivia, she purified the air of disease! I instantly turned into a dear. Desire for her stalked me like dangerous and cruel hunting dogs.
[The servant VALENTINE enters.]
What news do you bring of the Countess Olivia?

VALENTINE Sir, she refused to receive me. Her maidservant gave me a reply. The Countess will not appear outdoors for seven years. Like a nun, she will wear a veil and walk weeping about her room each day. She mourns to honor her dead brother, whom she loved.

DUKE O, she that hath a heart of that fine frame
To pay, this debt of love but to a brother,
How will she love, when the rich golden shaft
Hath kill'd the flock of all affections else
That live in her; when liver, brain, and heart,
These sovereign thrones, are all supplied, and fill'd
Her sweet perfections with one self king!
Away before me to sweet beds of flowers;
Love-thoughts lie rich when canopied with bowers.
[Exeunt]

DUKE She has a great heart to honor her brother with grief. She will be even more steadfast when Cupid's arrow erases all other devotion in her. Her inner organs will fill themselves with love for one man, her king. I am going to lie on flower beds. Thoughts of love are rich when shaded with leafy limbs. *[They all depart.]*

ACT I, SCENE 2

The seacoast.

[Enter VIOLA, a CAPTAIN, and Sailors]

VIOLA What country, friends, is this?

CAPTAIN This is Illyria, lady.

VIOLA And what should I do in Illyria?
My brother he is in Elysium.
Perchance he is not drown'd. What think you, sailors?

CAPTAIN It is perchance that you yourself were saved.

VIOLA Oh, my poor brother! and so perchance may he be.

CAPTAIN True, madam; and, to comfort you with chance,
Assure yourself, after our ship did split,
When you and those poor number saved with you
Hung on our driving boat, I saw your brother,
Most provident in peril, bind himself,
Courage and hope both teaching him the practice,
To a strong mast that lived upon the sea;
Where, like Arion on the dolphin's back,
I saw him hold acquaintance with the waves
So long as I could see.

VIOLA For saying so, there's gold.
Mine own escape unfoldeth to my hope,
Where to thy speech serves for authority,
The like of him. Know'st thou this country?

CAPTAIN Ay, madam, well; for I was bred and born
Not three hours' travel from this very place.

VIOLA Who governs here?

CAPTAIN A noble Duke, in nature as in name.

VIOLA What is his name?

CAPTAIN Orsino.

VIOLA Orsino! I have heard my father name him.
He was a bachelor then.

ACT I, SCENE 2

On Illyria's shore along the Adriatic Sea opposite Italy.

[VIOLA, a SEA CAPTAIN, and sailors enter.]

VIOLA Friends, where are we?

CAPTAIN Ma'am, this is Illyria.

VIOLA What should I do in Illyria? My brother is in heaven. Maybe he didn't drown. What do you sailors think of his chances of survival?

CAPTAIN He may have survived the way that you did.

VIOLA My poor brother, he may by luck still be alive.

CAPTAIN Yes, Viola. You may take comfort in this fact: After the ship split apart, when you and the other survivors clung to wreckage, I saw your brother. With bravery and hope, he tied himself to a mast that floated on the sea. Like Arion, the Greek boy whom a dolphin saved from drowning, your brother floated out of my sight.

VIOLA For your hopeful message, I reward you with gold coins. My survival and your observations support my hope that my brother also survived. Do you know anything about Illyria?

CAPTAIN Yes, ma'am. I was born and grew up less than three hours' journey from this beach.

VIOLA Who governs Illyria?

CAPTAIN A duke who is noble in behavior and in reputation.

VIOLA What is his name?

CAPTAIN Orsino.

VIOLA Orsino! I have heard my father speak of him. Orsino was then unmarried.

CAPTAIN And so is now, or was so very late;
For but a month ago I went from hence,
And then 'twas fresh in murmur,—as, you know,
What great ones do the less will prattle of,—
That he did seek the love of fair Olivia.

VIOLA What's she?

CAPTAIN A virtuous maid, the daughter of a count
That died some twelvenmonths since; then leaving her
In the protection of his son, her brother,
Who shortly also died: for whose dear love,
They say, she hath abjured the company
And sight of men.

VIOLA O that I
served that lady,
And might not be deliver'd to the world,
Till I had made mine own occasion mellow,
What my estate is!

CAPTAIN That were hard to compass,
Because she will admit no kind of suit,
No, not the duke's.

VIOLA There is a fair behaviour in thee, captain;
And though that nature with a beauteous wall
Doth oft close in pollution, yet of thee
I will believe thou hast a mind that suits
With this thy fair and outward character.
I prithee, and I'll pay thee bounteously,
Conceal me what I am, and be my aid
For such disguise as haply shall become
The form of my intent. I'll serve this Duke;
Thou shalt present me as an eunuch to him.
It may be worth thy pains; for I can sing
And speak to him in many sorts of music,
That will allow me very worth his service.
What else may hap to time I will commit;
Only shape thou thy silence to my wit.

CAPTAIN Be you his eunuch, and your mute I'll be.
When my tongue blabs, then let mine eyes not see.

VIOLA I thank thee; lead me on.
[Exeunt]

CAPTAIN The last I heard, Orsino was still a bachelor. I sailed from here a month ago. Rumor then declared Orsino in love with the Countess Olivia. Peasants love to gossip about rulers.

VIOLA Describe her.

CAPTAIN A decent woman, the daughter of a count who died a year ago. He left her in the care of his son, who recently died. Because she loved her brother, she has sworn off male visitors.

VIOLA I would love to serve the countess. I would stay with her until I decided what I will do with myself.

CAPTAIN That would be difficult to arrange. She conducts no business, not even with Duke Orsino.

VIOLA You are a kind man, Captain. Even though nature covers ugliness with pretty surroundings, I believe that your character is as handsome as your behavior. Please, let me pay for your help. Hide my identity and help me disguise my purpose. I will serve Duke Orsino. Introduce me to him as a eunuch. I will reward you. I can alter my voice to sound like a eunuch. He will accept me as a servant. I leave the rest up to luck. Please keep my secret.

CAPTAIN Act the part of eunuch and I will keep your secret. If I talk too much, let my eyes see nothing to report.

VIOLA Thank you. Lead me ashore. *[They depart.]*

ACT I, SCENE 3

A room in Olivia's house.

[Enter SIR TOBY BELCH and MARIA]

SIR TOBY What a plague means my niece, to take the death of her brother thus? I am sure care's an enemy to life.

MARIA By my troth, Sir Toby, you must come in earlier o' nights. Your cousin, my lady, takes great exceptions to your ill hours.

SIR TOBY Why, let her except, before excepted.

MARIA Ay, but you must confine yourself within the modest limits of order.

SIR TOBY Confine! I'll confine myself no finer than I am. These clothes are good enough to drink in; and so be these boots too. An they be not, let them hang themselves in their own straps.

MARIA That quaffing and drinking will undo you. I heard my lady talk of it yesterday; and of a foolish knight that you brought in one night here to be her wooer.

SIR TOBY Who, Sir Andrew Aguecheek?

MARIA Ay, he.

SIR TOBY He's as tall a man as any's in Illyria.

MARIA What's that to the purpose?

SIR TOBY Why, he has three thousand ducats a year.

MARIA Ay, but he'll have but a year in all these ducats; he's a very fool and a prodigal.

SIR TOBY Fie, that you'll say so! He plays o' the viol-de-gamboys, and speaks three or four languages word for word without book, and hath all the good gifts of nature.

MARIA He hath indeed, almost natural: for besides that he's a fool, he's a great quarreller; and but that lie hath the gift of a coward to allay the gust he hath in quarrelling, 'tis thought among the prudent he would quickly have the gift of a grave.

ACT I, SCENE 3

A room in the residence of the Countess Olivia.

[SIR TOBY BELCH and MARIA enter.]

SIR TOBY What harm does my niece mean by mourning her brother for seven years. I am certain that grief endangers her life.

MARIA Truly, Sir Toby, you must stop keeping late hours. Your niece, the Countess Olivia, disapproves of your late nights.

SIR TOBY Let her complain. I don't care.

MARIA You should limit your carousing.

SIR TOBY Control! I want no part of control. I wear suitable clothes for barrooms. My boots are also suitable. If they are unworthy, let them hang themselves on nooses made from bootlaces.

MARIA You will die of boozing. The Countess mentioned your bad habits yesterday. She talked of the silly courtier you brought here one night to romance her.

SIR TOBY Are you referring to Sir Andrew Aguecheek?

MARIA Yes.

SIR TOBY He is as fine a man as any in Illyria.

MARIA What do you mean?

SIR TOBY He earns about $10,000 a year.

MARIA His money won't last out the year. He's a wasteful fool.

SIR TOBY Shame on you for saying that. He plays the violincello, speaks three or four languages fluently, and is naturally gifted.

MARIA He is truly an idiot. He's also a bumbler and a quibbler. His cowardice tempers his zest for arguing. Wise people think he will soon run himself into the grave.

SIR TOBY By this hand, they are scoundrels and substractors that say so of him. Who are they?

MARIA They that add, moreover, he's drunk nightly in your company.

SIR TOBY With drinking healths to my niece. I'll drink to her as long as there is a passage in my throat and drink in Illyria. He's a coward and a coystrill that will not drink to my niece till his brains turn o' the toe like a parish-top. What, wench! Castiliano vulgo! for here comes sir Andrew Agueface.

[Enter SIR ANDREW AGUECHEEK]

SIR ANDREW Sir Toby Belch! how now, Sir Toby Belch!

SIR TOBY Sweet Sir Andrew!

SIR ANDREW Bless you, fair shrew.

MARIA And you too, sir.

SIR TOBY Accost, Sir Andrew, accost.

SIR ANDREW What's that?

SIR TOBY My niece's chamber-maid.

SIR ANDREW Good Mistress Accost, I desire better acquaintance.

MARIA My name is Mary, sir.

SIR ANDREW Good Mistress Mary Accost,—

SIR TOBY You mistake, knight: accost is, front her, board her, woo her, assail her.

SIR ANDREW By my troth, I would not undertake her in this company. Is that the meaning of accost?

MARIA Fare you well, gentlemen.

SIR TOBY An thou let part so, Sir Andrew, would thou mightst never draw sword again.

SIR ANDREW An you part so, mistress, I would I might never draw sword again. Fair lady, do you think you have fools in hand?

MARIA Sir, I have not you by the hand.

SIR ANDREW Marry, but you shall have; and here's my hand.

SIR TOBY	I swear, only rascals and defamers say that of Sir Andrew Aguecheek. Who told you that?
MARIA	The same people say that you and Sir Andrew get drunk every night.
SIR TOBY	I drink to the health of my niece Olivia. I will salute her so long as I can swallow and there is alcohol in Illyria. Anybody who refuses to drink to the Countess until his head whirls like a top is a wretch and a rascal. Look woman—peasant from Castile—Here is Sir Andrew Jawthrob. *[SIR ANDREW AGUECHEEK enters.]*
SIR ANDREW	Sir Toby Belch! How are you?
SIR TOBY	Dear Sir Andrew!
SIR ANDREW	Blessings on you, pretty scold.
MARIA	And on you, sir.
SIR TOBY	Speak to Maria, Sir Andrew.
SIR ANDREW	What?
SIR TOBY	Speak to Maria, who is Olivia's chambermaid.
SIR ANDREW	Miss Accost, I would like to know you better.
MARIA	My name is Mary, sir.
SIR ANDREW	Miss Mary Accost,
SIR TOBY	You misunderstand me, sir. By "accost," I mean converse with her, embrace her, court her, romance her.
SIR ANDREW	I wouldn't do that in public. Is that what "accost" means?
MARIA	Goodbye, gentlemen.
SIR TOBY	If you let her go like this, Sir Andrew, may you never draw your sword again.
SIR ANDREW	If you leave now, Miss, I hope never to draw my sword again. Fair Maria, do you think you are talking to fools?
MARIA	Sir, I am not talking to you.
SIR ANDREW	But you will. Here's my hand.

MARIA Now, sir, thought is free. I pray you, bring your hand to the butter-bar and let it drink.

SIR ANDREW Wherefore, sweetheart? what's your metaphor?

MARIA It's dry, sir.

SIR ANDREW Why, I think so; I am not such an ass but I can keep my hand dry. But what's your jest?

MARIA A dry jest, sir.

SIR ANDREW Are you full of them?

MARIA Ay, sir; I have them at my fingers' ends: marry, now I let go your hand I am barren. *[Exit MARIA]*

SIR TOBY O knight, thou lackest a cup of canary. When did I see thee so put down?

SIR ANDREW Never in your life, I think, unless you see canary put me down. Methinks sometimes I have no more wit than a Christian or an ordinary man has; but I am a great eater of beef, and I believe that does harm to my wit.

SIR TOBY No question.

SIR ANDREW An I thought that, I'd forswear it. I'll ride home to-morrow, Sir Toby.

SIR TOBY Pourquoi, my dear knight?

SIR ANDREW What is "pourquoi"? do or not do? I would I had bestowed that time in the tongues that I have in fencing, dancing, and bear-baiting. O, had I but followed the arts!

SIR TOBY Then hadst thou had an excellent head of hair.

SIR ANDREW Why, would that have mended my hair?

SIR TOBY Past question, for thou seest it will not curl by nature.

SIR ANDREW But it becomes me well enough, does't not?

SIR TOBY Excellent; it hangs like flax on a distaff.

SIR ANDREW Faith, I'll home to-morrow, Sir Toby. Your niece will not be seen; or if she be, it's four to one she'll none of me. The count himself here hard by woos her.

MARIA	Think whatever you want, sir. Come to the bar and pour a drink from the wine butts.
SIR ANDREW	What do you imply, dear? What is your meaning?
MARIA	It is droll wit, sir.
SIR ANDREW	It is truly droll. I am not so stupid that I can't dry my hand. What is the joke?
MARIA	A dull joke, sir.
SIR ANDREW	Do you like dry humor?
MARIA	Yes, sir. I keep it at my fingertips. When I drop your hand, I hold no more jokes. *[MARIA goes out.]*
SIR TOBY	Sir, you need a cup of sweet wine from the Canary Islands. I've never seen you so trounced in joking.
SIR ANDREW	I've never been so defeated unless I'm drunk on Canary wine. I am no funnier than any other man. I eat too much beef, which destroys intelligence.
SIR TOBY	I agree.
SIR ANDREW	If I believed that, I'd give up beef. I am going home tomorrow, Sir Toby.
SIR TOBY	Pourquoi, dear sir?
SIR ANDREW	What does "pourquoi" mean—ride home or not ride home? I wish I had studied French as much as I studied fencing, dancing, and bear fighting with hounds. I wish I had pursued the arts!
SIR TOBY	If so, you would have thick hair.
SIR ANDREW	How would the arts improve my hair?
SIR TOBY	Without question, it is not naturally curly.
SIR ANDREW	It looks good, doesn't it?
SIR TOBY	It is excellent. It hangs like linen thread on a spinner.
SIR ANDREW	I'm going home tomorrow, Sir Toby. The Countess Olivia won't see visitors. If she did accept guests, she wouldn't see me. Count Orsino who lives near here courts her.

SIR TOBY She'll none o' the count. She'll not match above her degree, neither in estate, years, nor wit. I have heard her swear't. Tut, there's life in't, man.

SIR ANDREW I'll stay a month longer. I am a fellow o' the strangest mind i' the world; I delight in masques and revels sometimes altogether.

SIR TOBY Art thou good at these kickshawses, knight?

SIR ANDREW As any man in Illyria, whatsoever he be, under the degree of my betters; and yet I will not compare with an old man.

SIR TOBY What is thy excellence in a galliard, knight?

SIR ANDREW Faith, I can cut a caper.

SIR TOBY And I can cut the mutton to't.

SIR ANDREW And I think I have the back-trick simply as strong as any man in Illyria.

SIR TOBY Wherefore are these things hid? where fore have these gifts a curtain before 'em? are they like to take dust, like Mistress Mall's picture? why dost thou not go to church in a galliard and come home in a coranto? My very walk should be a jig. I would not so much as make water but in a sink-a-pace. What dost thou mean? Is it a world to hide virtues in? I did think, by the excellent constitution of thy leg, it was formed under a star of a galliard.

SIR ANDREW Ay, 'tis strong, and it does indifferent well in a flame-coloured stock. Shall we set about some revels?

SIR TOBY What shall we do else? were we not born under Taurus?

SIR ANDREW Taurus! That's sides and heart.

SIR TOBY No, sir; it is legs and thighs. Let me see thee caper. Ha! higher; ha, ha! excellent!
[Exeunt]

SIR TOBY	She rejects Orsino. She won't have any man who outranks her in property, age, or intelligence. I've heard her say so. You might have a chance.
SIR ANDREW	I will stay another month. I have unusual tastes. I like drama and entertainments, sometimes both at once.
SIR TOBY	Are you talented at these amusements, sir?
SIR ANDREW	Like anybody in Illyria who is no more aristocratic than I. I won't compare my dancing to a more experienced man.
SIR TOBY	Can you dance a jig, sir?
SIR ANDREW	Yes, I can leap about.
SIR TOBY	And I can cut mutton to go with caper sauce.
SIR ANDREW	I can do a back flip as well as any man in Illyria.
SIR TOBY	Why do you hide these accomplishments? Why do you conceal your talents? Are they covered in dust, like a portrait behind a curtain? Why not go to church with a jigging step and come home at a run? If it were me, I would walk in triple time. I don't even urinate except in a five-step dance. Why are you shy? Should anybody conceal talents? I guessed that your fine leg was the result of dancing.
SIR ANDREW	Yes, it's strong. And it looks good in a red stocking. Shall we try some amusements?
SIR TOBY	Of course. Were we not born under the sign of the bull, controller of the legs?
SIR ANDREW	Taurus controls the sides and heart.
SIR TOBY	You're wrong. Taurus controls the legs and thighs. Let me see you leap. Yes, go higher. Yes, yes! Excellent! *[SIR TOBY and SIR ANDREW depart.]*

ACT I, SCENE 4

The Duke's palace.

[Enter VALENTINE, and VIOLA in man's attire]

VALENTINE If the duke continue these favours towards you, Cesario, you are like to be much advanced. He hath known you but three days, and already you are no stranger.

VIOLA You either fear his humour or my negligence that you call in question the continuance of his love. Is he inconstant, sir, in his favours?

VALENTINE No, believe me.

VIOLA I thank you. Here comes the count.
[Enter DUKE, CURIO, and Attendants]

DUKE Who saw Cesario, ho?

VIOLA On your attendance, my lord; here.

DUKE Stand you a while aloof. Cesario,
Thou know'st no less but all. I have unclasp'd
To thee the book even of my secret soul;
Therefore, good youth, address thy gait unto her;
Be not denied access, stand at her doors,
And tell them, there thy fixed foot shall grow
Till thou have audience.

VIOLA Sure, my noble lord,
If she be so abandon'd to her sorrow
As it is spoke, she never will admit me.

DUKE Be clamorous and leap all civil bounds
Rather than make unprofited return.

VIOLA Say I do speak with her, my lord, what then?

DUKE Oh, then unfold the passion of my love,
Surprise her with discourse of my dear faith
It shall become thee well to act my woes;
She will attend it better in thy youth
Than in a nuncio's of more grave aspect.

VIOLA I think not so, my lord.

ACT I, SCENE 4

At Duke Orsino's palace.

[VALENTINE enters with VIOLA, who is dressed like a man and travels under the name CESARIO.]

VALENTINE If you continue pleasing Count Orsino, Cesario, he may promote you. In only three days, he is familiar with you.

VIOLA You either fear his whim or my failure. You doubt he will continue preferring my service. Is he wishy-washy in his preferences?

VALENTINE No, trust me.

VIOLA Thank you. Here comes Count Orsino. *[DUKE ORSINO, CURIO, and servants enter.]*

DUKE Where is Cesario?

VIOLA Here at your service, sir.

DUKE Leave us in private. Cesario, you are knowledgeable. I have revealed to you my inner secrets. So, dear boy, go to Countess Olivia. If she won't let you in, stay at the entrance. Tell her staff that you won't move until she agrees to see you.

VIOLA Certainly, my lord. If she is as deep in sorrow as she said, she won't see me.

DUKE Raise an uproar. Violate courtesy rather than return without seeing her.

VIOLA If I see her, Duke Orsino, what should I say to her?

DUKE Tell her how deeply I admire her. Impress her with a narrative of my sincerity. Demonstrate my lovesickness. She will listen better to a boy than to an older messenger.

VIOLA I disagree, sir.

DUKE Dear lad, believe it;
For they shall yet belie thy happy years,
That say thou art a man. Diana's lip
Is not more smooth and rubious; thy small pipe
Is as the maiden's organ, shrill and sound;
And all is semblative a woman's part
I know thy constellation is right apt
For this affair. Some four or five attend him,
All, if you will; for I myself am best
When least in company. Prosper well in this,
And thou shalt live as freely as thy lord,
To call his fortunes thine.

VIOLA I'll do my best
To woo your lady; *[aside]* yet, a barful strife!
Whoe'er I woo, myself would be his wife.
[Exeunt]

DUKE Trust me, boy. Anyone who thinks you are a grown man lies. Your lips are smoother and redder than the goddess Diana. Your voice is light and true as a girl's. You are so like a woman that I know you are right for this assignment. Four or five of you servents go with Cesario. All may go if you want. I am better at talking one-to-one. Do a good job. You will live as well as your master and share his wealth.

VIOLA I will court Countess Olivia as well as I can. *[Speaking to herself.]* This is a course full of obstacles! Whatever woman I court for Duke Orsino, I would like to marry him myself. *[They depart.]*

ACT I, SCENE 5

Olivia's house.

[Enter MARIA and CLOWN]

MARIA Nay, either tell me where thou hast been, or I will not open my lips so wide as a bristle may enter in way of thy excuse. My lady will hang thee for thy absence.

CLOWN Let her hang me; he that is well hanged in this world needs to fear no colours.

MARIA Make that good.

CLOWN He shall see none to fear.

MARIA A good lenten answer. I can tell thee where that saying was born, of "I fear no colours."

CLOWN Where, good Mistress Mary?

MARIA In the wars; and that may you be bold to say in your foolery.

CLOWN Well, God give them wisdom that have it; and those that are fools, let them use their talents.

MARIA Yet you will be hanged for being so long absent; or, to be turned away, is not that as good as a hanging to you?

CLOWN Many a good hanging prevents a bad marriage; and, for turning away, let summer bear it out.

MARIA You are resolute, then?

CLOWN Not so, neither; but I am resolved on two points.

MARIA That if one break, the other will hold; or, if both break, your gaskins fall.

CLOWN Apt, in good faith, very apt. Well, go thy way; if Sir Toby would leave drinking, thou wert as witty a piece of Eve's flesh as any in Illyria.

MARIA Peace, you rogue, no more o' that. Here comes my lady. Make your excuse wisely, you were best.

[Exit]

ACT I, SCENE 5

The residence of the Countess Olivia.

[MARIA and the jester FESTE enter.]

MARIA Tell me where you have been or I won't open my mouth wider than a toothbrush bristle to excuse your absence. The Countess Olivia will send you to the gallows for leaving without permission.

CLOWN Let her execute me. He who goes to the gallows has no fear of enemy flags.

MARIA Prove it.

CLOWN He shall see nothing to fear.

MARIA A limp reply. I know the source of the saying "I fear no flags."

CLOWN What is the source, Maria?

MARIA In the wars. You are sassy in your jesting.

CLOWN God blessed some people with wisdom. Those who are born fools must use the talents they have.

MARIA You will be hanged for disappearing from service. Isn't a dismissal as good as execution to you?

CLOWN Execution may prevent a bad marriage. And as to losing my job, I can live through the summer.

MARIA You won't change your mind?

CLOWN No. I have two reasons for making up my mind.

MARIA If one point breaks, you can rely on the other. If both points fail, your pants will fall down.

CLOWN Clever, very clever. Leave me. If you could lure Sir Toby from alcohol, you would be the finest wife in Illyria.

MARIA Hush, you rascal, don't say that. Here comes the Countess Olivia. You would be wise to make a believable excuse. *[MARIA departs.]*

CLOWN Wit, an't be thy will, put me into good fooling! Those wits, that think they have thee, do very oft prove fools; and I, that am sure I lack thee, may pass for a wise man. For what says Quinapalus? "Better a witty fool than a foolish wit."
[Enter LADY OLIVIA with MALVOLIO]
God bless thee, lady!

OLIVIA Take the fool away.

CLOWN Do you not hear, fellows? Take away the lady.

OLIVIA Go to, you're a dry fool; I'll no more of you. Besides, you grow dishonest.

CLOWN Two faults, madonna, that drink and good counsel will amend: for give the dry fool drink, then is the fool not dry; bid the dishonest man mend himself; if he mend, he is no longer dishonest; if he cannot, let the botcher mend him. Anything that's mended is but patched: virtue that transgresses is but patched with sin; and sin that amends is but patched with virtue. If that this simple syllogism will serve, so; if it will not, what remedy? The lady bade take away the fool; therefore, I say again, take her away.

OLIVIA Sir, I bade them take away you.

CLOWN Misprision in the highest degree! Lady, cucullus non facit monachum. That's as much to say as I wear not motley in my brain. Good madonna, give me leave to prove you a fool.

OLIVIA Can you do it?

CLOWN Dexteriously, good madonna.

OLIVIA Make your proof.

CLOWN I must catechize you for it, madonna. Good my mouse of virtue, answer me.

OLIVIA Well, sir, for want of other idleness, I'll bide your proof.

CLOWN Good madonna, why mournest thou?

OLIVIA Good fool, for my brother's death.

CLOWN I think his soul is in hell, madonna.

OLIVIA I know his soul is in heaven, fool.

CLOWN Brain, please help me fool her. The wits I depend on often prove false. And I, a fool, often pass for smart. What does Quinapalus say on the matter? It is better to be a chatty idiot than a stupid intellectual. *[The COUNTESS OLIVIA enters with MALVOLIO.]* God bless you, Countess Olivia.

OLIVIA Remove this idiot.

CLOWN Don't you understand, men? Remove the Countess.

OLIVIA Go away. You're a stupid dullard. I want you to leave. And you have become unreliable.

CLOWN My lady, I can repair those two faults with drinking and wise advice. If I give a stupid dolt a drink, then he is no longer a dry fool. Let the unreliable man cure himself. If he improves, he will no longer be unreliable. If he can't fix his bad habits, let the tailor's patcher fix him. Anything that is repaired is patchwork. Goodness that does wrong wears sin like patches. Any wrongdoing that improves is only patched goodness. If this basic logic explains things, it is good. If there are still questions, how can I fix it? The Countess ordered the men to remove the idiot. Thus, I repeat, take away the Countess.

OLIVIA Sir, I ordered them to remove you.

CLOWN The worst of misunderstandings! Countess, a hooded robe does not make a man a monk. By that I mean, my clown suit does not cover my brain. My lady, let me prove you stupid.

OLIVIA Can you do it?

CLOWN Easily, my lady.

OLIVIA Prove it.

CLOWN I must question you, my lady. My darling good lady, tell me.

OLIVIA Since I have nothing else to do, I will humor you.

CLOWN My lady, why do you grieve?

OLIVIA Stupid man, I am sad about my brother's death.

CLOWN I think his soul has gone to hell, my lady.

OLIVIA Idiot, I know his soul has gone to heaven.

CLOWN The more fool, madonna, to mourn for your brother's soul being in heaven. Take away the fool, gentlemen.

OLIVIA What think you of this fool, Malvolio? Doth he not mend?

MALVOLIO Yes, and shall do till the pangs of death shake him. Infirmity, that decays the wise, doth ever make the better fool.

CLOWN God send you sir, a speedy infirmity, for the better increasing your folly! Sir Toby will be sworn that I am no fox; but he will not pass his word for two pence that you are no fool.

OLIVIA How say you to that, Malvolio?

MALVOLIO I marvel your ladyship takes delight in such a barren rascal. I saw him put down the other day with an ordinary fool that has no more brain than a stone. Look you now, he's out of his guard already. Unless you laugh and minister occasion to him, he is gagged. I protest, I take these wise men, that crow so at these set kind of fools, no better than the fools' zanies.

OLIVIA O, you are sick of self-love, Malvolio, and taste with a distempered appetite. To be generous, guiltless, and of free disposition, is to take those things for bird-bolts that you deem cannon-bullets. There is no slander in an allowed fool, though he do nothing but rail; nor no railing in a known discreet man, though he do nothing but reprove.

CLOWN Now Mercury endue thee with leasing, for thou speakest well of fools!
[Re-enter MARIA]

MARIA Madam, there is at the gate a young gentleman much desires to speak with you.

OLIVIA From the Count Orsino, is it?

MARIA I know not, madam; 'tis a fair young man, and well attended.

OLIVIA Who of my people hold him in delay?

MARIA Sir Toby, madam, your kinsman.

CLOWN Then you are foolish, my lady, for grieving after your brother's soul has gone to heaven. Gentlemen, remove the Countess for being a fool.

OLIVIA Malvolio, what is your opinion of this joker? Is he improving?

MALVOLIO Yes, and he will go on improving to his dying day. Old age, which withers wise people, also makes them more foolish.

CLOWN God send you senility to worsen your foolishness more rapidly. Sir Toby will swear that I am not crafty. But he wouldn't take two pennies to say you are not stupid.

OLIVIA What do you think of that, Malvolio?

MALVOLIO I am surprised that your ladyship enjoys such an empty-headed rogue. I saw him ridiculed recently by an ordinary dullard who had no more sense than a stone. Look at him now. He is speechless already. Unless you laugh at his joke and give him a chance to recover, he can't speak. I declare that intelligent people who laugh at comedians are no better than the jesters of clowns.

OLIVIA Oh, Malvolio, you are stuffed with ego. You digest with an upset stomach. You would be generous, blameless, and comfortable to take for blunt darts the words you claim to be cannon balls. A professional comic causes no insult. He only raves. Wise men cause no harm, even though they constantly scold.

CLOWN May the god Mercury bless you with a liar's art. How dare you compliment fools! *[MARIA returns.]*

MARIA A young man at the entrance wants to talk with you, ma'am.

OLIVIA Did he come from Count Orsino?

MARIA I don't know, ma'am. He is a handsome youth accompanied by servants.

OLIVIA Which of my staff is at the door with him?

MARIA Your relative, Sir Toby, ma'am.

OLIVIA Fetch him off, I pray you; he speaks nothing but madman; fie on him! *[Exit Maria]* Go you, Malvolio. If it be a suit from the count, I am sick, or not at home—what you will, to dismiss it. *[Exit Malvolio]* Now you see, sir, how your fooling grows old, and people dislike it.

CLOWN Thou hast spoke for us, madonna, as if thy eldest son should be a fool, whose skull Jove cram with brains! for,—here he comes,—one of thy kin has a most weak pia mater.
[Enter SIR TOBY]

OLIVIA By mine honour, half drunk. What is he at the gate, cousin?

SIR TOBY A gentleman.

OLIVIA A gentleman! what gentleman?

SIR TOBY 'Tis a gentleman here—a plague o' these pickle-herring! How now, sot!

CLOWN Good Sir Toby!

OLIVIA Cousin, cousin, how have you come so early by this lethargy?

SIR TOBY Lechery? I defy lechery. There's one at the gate.

OLIVIA Ay, marry, what is he?

SIR TOBY Let him be the devil, an he will, I care not. Give me faith, say I. Well, it's all one.
[Exit]

OLIVIA What's a drunken man like, fool?

CLOWN Like a drowned man, a fool, and a madman: one draught above heat makes a fool; the second mads him; and a third drowns him.

OLIVIA Go thou and seek the crowner, and let him sit o' my coz; for he's in the third degree of drink, he's drowned. Go, look after him.

CLOWN He is but mad yet, madonna; and the fool shall look to the madman.
[Exit]
[Re-enter MALVOLIO]

OLIVIA Please, send Sir Toby away. He talks like a lunatic. Shame on him. *[MARIA goes out.]* Malvolio, you go to the door. If it is a message from Duke Orsino, say I am ill or not at home. Say whatever you want to get rid of the messenger. *[MALVOLIO goes out.]* Now you understand how your foolery bores and wearies people.

CLOWN You speak for all of us, my lady. As if your oldest son should be stupid after Jupiter stuffed his head with brains! Here comes Sir Toby, a relative of yours with the weakest brain. *[SIR TOBY enters.]*

OLIVIA I declare, Sir Toby is half drunk. Who waits at the gate, Sir Toby?

SIR TOBY A gentleman.

OLIVIA A gentleman! What gentleman?

SIR TOBY A gentleman has come. I am ill from eating pickled herring! How are you, nitwit!

CLOWN Sir Toby!

OLIVIA Kinsman, why are you drunk so early in the day?

SIR TOBY Lust? I am not lustful. There is someone at the gate.

OLIVIA Who is it?

SIR TOBY I wouldn't care if it were Satan. Strengthen my faith, I say. It doesn't matter. *[SIR TOBY departs.}*

OLIVIA How would you describe a drunk, jester?

CLOWN A drunk is like a drowning victim, an idiot, and a madman. One drink makes him an idiot. The second drink drives him crazy. He drowns in the third drink.

OLIVIA Send for the coroner. Let him judge my kinsman Toby. Toby's reached the third stage of drunkenness. He has drowned in alcohol. Go tend to him.

CLOWN He is only insane, my lady. An idiot can tend to a crazy man. *[The clown FESTE departs.]*
[MALVOLIO returns.]

MALVOLIO Madam, yond young fellow swears he will speak with you. I told him you were sick; he takes on him to understand so much, and therefore comes to speak with you. I told him you were asleep; he seems to have a foreknowledge of that too, and therefore comes to speak with you. What is to be said to him, lady? He's fortified against any denial.

OLIVIA Tell him he shall not speak with me.

MALVOLIO Has been told so; and he says, he'll stand at your door like a sheriff's post, and be the supporter to a bench, but he'll speak with you.

OLIVIA What kind o' man is he?

MALVOLIO Why, of mankind.

OLIVIA What manner of man?

MALVOLIO Of very ill manner; he'll speak with you, will you or no.

OLIVIA Of what personage and years is he?

MALVOLIO Not yet old enough for a man, nor young enough for a boy; as a squash is before 'tis a peascod, or a codling when 'tis almost an apple. 'Tis with him in standing water, between boy and man. He is very well favoured and he speaks very shrewishly; one would think his mother's milk were scarce out of him.

OLIVIA Let him approach. Call in my gentlewoman.

MALVOLIO Gentlewoman, my lady calls.
[Exit]
[Re-enter MARIA]

OLIVIA Give me my veil. Come throw it o'er my face.
We'll once more hear Orsino's embassy.
[Enter VIOLA and Attendants]

VIOLA The honourable lady of the house, which is she?

OLIVIA Speak to me; I shall answer for her. Your will?

MALVOLIO Madam, the young messenger insists on speaking to you. I told him you were ill. He pretends to be knowledgeable and wants to talk with you. I told him you were sleeping. He refuses to be fooled by that excuse and insists on speaking with you. What shall I tell him, Countess? He is prepared for every excuse.

OLIVIA Tell him he can't see me.

MALVOLIO I told him. He declares that he will stay at your door like a sheriff's deputy. He will be a leg on the judge's bench. But he insists on seeing you.

OLIVIA What sort of person is he?

MALVOLIO Human.

OLIVIA How does he behave?

MALVOLIO He is discourteous. He will talk to you whether you like it or not.

OLIVIA Describe his appearance and age.

MALVOLIO He is between man and boy. Like a green peapod before it ripens, or a green apple before it turns red. He is like the ocean between tides, between childhood and manhood. He is attractive. He speaks sharply. He acts like a newly weaned child.

OLIVIA Let him come in. Summon my maid.

MALVOLIO Maria, the Countess needs you. *[MALVOLIO departs.]* *[MARIA returns.]*

OLIVIA Hand me my mourner's veil. Drape it over my face. We will hear another messenger from Count Orsino. *[VIOLA and servants enter COUNTESS OLIVIA's home.]*

VIOLA Point out the lady of the house.

OLIVIA Address your questions to me. I will speak for the Countess. What do you want?

VIOLA Most radiant, exquisite and unmatchable beauty, —I pray you, tell me if this be the lady of the house, for I never saw her. I would be loath to cast away my speech, for besides that it is excellently well penned, I have taken great pains to con it. Good beauties, let me sustain no scorn; I am very comptible, even to the least sinister usage.

OLIVIA Whence came you sir?

VIOLA I can say little more than I have studied, and that question's out of my part. Good gentle one, give me modest assurance if you be the lady of the house, that I may proceed in my speech.

OLIVIA Are you a comedian?

VIOLA No my profound heart; and yet by the very fangs of malice I swear, I am not that I play. Are you the lady of the house?

OLIVIA If I do not usurp myself, I am.

VIOLA Most certain, if you are she, you do usurp yourself; for what is yours to bestow is not yours to reserve. But this is from my commission. I will on with my speech in your praise, and then show you the heart of my message.

OLIVIA Come to what is important in't; I forgive you the praise.

VIOLA Alas, I took great pains to study it, and 'tis poetical.

OLIVIA It is the more like to be feigned; I pray you, keep it in. I heard you were saucy at my gates, and allowed your approach rather to wonder at you than to hear you. If you be not mad, be gone; if you have reason, be brief. 'Tis not that time of moon with me to make one in so skipping a dialogue.

MARIA Will you hoist sail, sir? here lies your way.

VIOLA No, good swabber; I am to hull here a little longer. Some mollification for your giant, sweet lady. Tell me your mind. I am a messenger.

OLIVIA Sure, you have some hideous matter to deliver, when the courtesy of it is so fearful. Speak your office.

VIOLA Most glowing, excellent, and unparalleled beauty. Please, identify the lady of the house. I have never seen her. I would hate to waste my prepared speech. It is beautifully composed. I worked hard to memorize it. Beautiful women, don't laugh at me. I am sensitive to the smallest form of ridicule.

OLIVIA Where did you come from, sir?

VIOLA I can only tell you what I memorized. That question is not part of the text. If you are the lady of the house, identify yourself so I may deliver my speech.

OLIVIA Are you a joker?

VIOLA No, by the depth of my heart. I declare by the teeth of evil that I am not an imposter. Are you the Countess Olivia?

OLIVIA If I do not presume too much, I am the lady of the house.

VIOLA If you are the Countess Olivia, you do presume too much. The virginity you treasure is not yours to keep. But I stray from my job. I will deliver my praise to you. Then I will tell you the purpose of my coming.

OLIVIA Come to the point. I will bypass the compliments.

VIOLA I worked hard to memorize it. It is poetry.

OLIVIA All the more reason to think it insincere. Please, don't tell me. I heard that you sassed the servants at the entrance. You tried to dazzle them rather than to speak plainly. If you aren't daft, go away. If you have sense, get to the point. It is not the phase of the moon when I would go crazy from not hearing your speech.

MARIA Will you shove off, sir? This is the way out.

VIOLA No, good deck scrubber. I must harbor here a while longer. Please gentle your bodyguard, sweet Countess. What do you choose? I have a message for you.

OLIVIA You must have some terrible news if you require so much preparation. Deliver your message.

VIOLA It alone concerns your ear. I bring no overture of war, no taxation of homage. I hold the olive in my hand; my words are as full of peace as matter.

OLIVIA Yet you began rudely. What are you? What would you?

VIOLA The rudeness that hath appeared in me have I learned from my entertainment. What I am, and what I would, are as secret as maidenhead; to your ears, divinity; to any other's, profanation.

OLIVIA Give us the place alone; we will hear this divinity.
[Exeunt MARIA and Attendants]
Now, sir, what is your text?

VIOLA Most sweet lady,—

OLIVIA A comfortable doctrine, and much may be said of it. Where lies your text?

VIOLA In Orsino's bosom.

OLIVIA In his bosom! In what chapter of his bosom?

VIOLA To answer by the method, in the first of his heart.

OLIVIA Oh, I have read it; it is heresy. Have you no more to say?

VIOLA Good madam, let me see your face.

OLIVIA Have you any commission from your lord to negotiate with my face? You are now out of your text; but we will draw the curtain and show you the picture. Look you, sir, such a one I was this present. Is't not well done? *[Unveiling]*

VIOLA Excellently done, if God did all.

OLIVIA 'Tis in grain sir; 'twill endure wind and weather.

VIOLA 'Tis beauty truly blent, whose red and white
Nature's own sweet and cunning hand laid on.
Lady, you are the cruell'st she alive,
If you will lead these graces to the grave
And leave the world no copy.

OLIVIA Oh, sir, I will not be so hard-hearted; I will give out divers schedules of my beauty. It shall be inventoried, and every particle and utensil labelled to my will: as, item, two lips, indifferent red; item, two grey eyes, with lids to them; item, one neck, one chin, and so forth. Were you sent hither to praise me?

VIOLA It concerns only you. I don't want to cause hostility or to demand any tribute. I come in peace. My speech is as peaceful as it is important.

OLIVIA Yet you were rude when you began. Who are you? What do you want?

VIOLA I was rude at first because your staff treated me crudely. What I am and what I want are as personal as virginity. To you, my words are sacred. To other listeners, my words violate your dignity.

OLIVIA Leave us in private. I want to hear these sacred words. *[MARIA and servants depart.]* Now, what do you have to say?

VIOLA Dear lady . . .

OLIVIA A comforting beginning worth praising. Where do these words come from?

VIOLA From Duke Orsino's heart.

OLIVIA From his heart? In what section of his heart?

VIOLA To answer like a minister delivering a sermon, his words come from the top of his heart.

OLIVIA I have read this sermon. It is false. Is that all you have to say?

VIOLA May I look on your face, ma'am?

OLIVIA Did Duke Orsino tell you to speak directly to my face? You have departed from your speech. I will remove the veil and show you my face. This is exactly how I look at the moment. Isn't it well done? *[Revealing her face]*

VIOLA Beautiful, if you wear no makeup.

OLIVIA My looks won't wash off, sir. This face will survive wind and weather.

VIOLA Your beauty is natural. It shows the rosy and creamy tones you were born with. Countess, you would be the harshest of women if you died without leaving the world a human copy of your loveliness.

OLIVIA I won't be cruel. I will list my assets. I will post in my will a labeled inventory of each physical feature. I will list two lips of ordinary red, two gray eyes with lids, one neck, one chin, and so forth. Did the Duke send you to evaluate me?

VIOLA I see you what you are, you are too proud;
But, if you were the devil, you are fair.
My lord and master loves you. O, such love
Could be but recompensed, though you were crown'd
The nonpareil of beauty!

OLIVIA How does he love me?

VIOLA With adorations, fertile tears,
With groans that thunder love, with sighs of fire.

OLIVIA Your lord does know my mind. I cannot love him;
Yet I suppose him virtuous, know him noble,
Of great estate, of fresh and stainless youth;
In voices well divulged, free, learn'd and valiant;
And in dimension and the shape of nature
A gracious person: but yet I cannot love him;
He might have took his answer long ago.

VIOLA If I did love you in my master's flame,
With such a suffering, such a deadly life,
In your denial I would find no sense;
I would not understand it.

OLIVIA Why, what would you?

VIOLA Make me a willow cabin at your gate,
And call upon my soul within the house;
Write loyal cantons of contemned love
And sing them loud even in the dead of night;
Halloo your name to the reverberate hills,
And make the babbling gossip of the air
Cry out 'Olivia!' Oh, you should not rest
Between the elements of air and earth,
But you should pity me!

OLIVIA You might do much. What is your parentage?

VIOLA Above my fortunes, yet my state is well;
I am a gentleman.

OLIVIA Get you to your lord;
I cannot love him. Let him send no more;
Unless, perchance, you come to me again,
To tell me how he takes it. Fare you well.
I thank you for your pains; spend this for me.

VIOLA I see now that you are too proud. But even if you were Satan, you are beautiful. My lord and master loves you. I wish you would return his love, even if you were crowned the most beautiful woman in the world.

OLIVIA How does he show his love?

VIOLA With admiration, constant weeping, outbursts of love, and ardent sighs.

OLIVIA Duke Orsino knows my reply. I can't love him. I assume he is good. I know he is noble, wealthy, a young man pure and sinless. According to reports, he is generous, educated, and brave. His physique and size are balanced. But I can't love him. He should have accepted my refusal long ago.

VIOLA If I adored you as deeply and passionately for the rest of my life, I would not comprehend your rejection. I would not understand.

OLIVIA What would you do?

VIOLA I would build a shelter of willow branches at your gate and call for you, my soul, to come out to me. I would compose love poems and sing them to you at night. I would shout your name and make it echo from the hills. I would fill the air with cries of "Olivia!" I would give you no rest so long as you were alive on this earth. I would make you pity me!

OLIVIA You might succeed. What family do you come from?

VIOLA They are more prestigious than my current state. But I live well. I am a gentleman.

OLIVIA Go back to Duke Orsino. I can't love him. Have him send no more messages. Unless you bring a report on how he responds to rejection. Good-bye. Thanks for trying so hard. Here are some coins.

VIOLA I am no fee'd post, lady; keep your purse.
My master, not myself, lacks recompense.
Love make his heart of flint that you shall love;
And let your fervour, like my master's, be
Placed in contempt! Farewell, fair cruelty.
[Exit]

OLIVIA 'What is your parentage?'
'Above my fortunes, yet my state is well;
I am a gentleman.' I'll be sworn thou art.
Thy tongue, thy face, thy limbs, actions, and spirit,
Do give thee five-fold blazon. Not too fast; soft, soft!
Unless the master were the man. How now!
Even so quickly may one catch the plague?
Methinks I feel this youth's perfections
With an invisible and subtle stealth
To creep in at mine eyes. Well, let it be.
What ho, Malvolio!
[Re-enter MALVOLIO]

MALVOLIO Here, madam, at your service.

OLIVIA Run after that same peevish messenger,
The county's man. He left this ring behind him,
Would I or not. Tell him I'll none of it.
Desire him not to flatter with his lord,
Nor hold him tip with hopes; I am not for him.
If that the youth will come this way to-morrow,
I'll give him reasons for't. Hie thee, Malvolio.

MALVOLIO Madam, I will.
[Exit]

OLIVIA I do I know not what, and fear to find
Mine eye too great a flatterer for my mind.
Fate, show thy force; ourselves we do not owe.
What is decreed must be, and be this so.
[Exit]

VIOLA I don't carry messages to earn money, Countess. Keep your money. It is Count Orsino, not me, whom you should pay. Because you reject him, his heart is as hard as flint. Let your refusal be scorned just as you scorn his ardent love. Goodbye, cruel beauty. *[VIOLA in the disguise of CESARIO departs.]*

OLIVIA "What family do you come from?" "They are more prestigious than my current state. But I live well. I am a gentleman." I am sure you are an aristocrat. Your words, appearance, shape, behavior, and spirit form a five-part coat of arms. I must go slowly. Carefully, carefully! Could Count Orsino be disguised as the messenger? Is it possible? Can a person fall ill with plague as easily as the messenger has touched me? This young man's qualities crept into my heart with unseen, subtle caution. Well, I can't do anything about it. Hey, Malvolio! *[MALVOLIO returns.]*

MALVOLIO I am here, ma'am, to serve you.

OLIVIA Overtake the messenger, Count Orsino's stubborn servant. The boy left this ring here against my wishes. Tell him I won't have it. Order him not to flatter me for Duke Orsino's sake or to hold the Duke on his fingertips in hope of winning me. I reject Duke Orsino. If the messenger will return tomorrow, I will explain my refusal. Hurry, Malvolio.

MALVOLIO I will, ma'am. *[MALVOLIO goes out.]*

OLIVIA I don't understand my actions. I am afraid that my brain allows my eyes to mislead me. Destiny, take charge of my life. People don't own themselves. What fate decrees for me must happen. I surrender myself to my destiny. *[COUNTESS OLIVIA goes out.]*

ACT II, SCENE 1

The seacoast.

[Enter ANTONIO and SEBASTIAN]

ANTONIO Will you stay no longer? nor will you not that I go with you?

SEBASTIAN By your patience, no. My stars shine darkly over me. The malignancy of my fate might perhaps distemper yours; therefore I shall crave of you your leave that I may bear my evils alone. It were a bad recompense for your love, to lay any of them on you.

ANTONIO Let me know of you whither you are bound.

SEBASTIAN No, sooth, sir. My determinate voyage is mere extravagancy. But I perceive in you so excellent a touch of modesty, that you will not extort from me what I am willing to keep in; therefore it charges me in manners the rather to express myself. You must know of me then, Antonio, my name is Sebastian, which I called Roderigo. My father was that Sebastian of Messaline, whom I know you have heard of. He left behind him myself and a sister, both born in an hour. If the heavens had been pleased, would we had so ended! But you, sir, altered that; for some hour before you took me from the breach of the sea was my sister drowned.

ANTONIO Alas the day!

SEBASTIAN A lady, sir, though it was said she much resembled me, was yet of many accounted beautiful; but, though I could not with such estimable wonder overfar believe that, yet thus far I will boldly publish her; she bore a mind that envy could not but call fair. She is drowned already, sir, with salt water, though I seem to drown her remembrance again with more.

ANTONIO Pardon me, sir, your bad entertainment.

SEBASTIAN O good Antonio, forgive me your trouble.

ANTONIO If you will not murder me for my love, let me be your servant.

ACT II, SCENE 1

On Illyria's shore along the Adriatic Sea opposite Italy.

[The sea captain ANTONIO and the youth SEBASTIAN enter.]

ANTONIO Won't you stay longer? Can't I go with you?

SEBASTIAN Please understand. No. Bad luck looms over me. Misfortune might descend on you, too. Please allow me to face my troubles alone. I would repay your friendship poorly by wishing bad luck on you.

ANTONIO Tell me where you are going.

SEBASTIAN I can't, sir. I am just wandering. I see such sensitivity in you that I know you won't force me to answer. My manners require that I say nothing. Antonio, my name is Sebastian. People call me Roderigo. My father was Sebastian of Messaline. I know you have heard of him. He died, leaving me and my twin sister. If God had allowed, I wish we, too, had died at the same time! But you saved me from dying. At the same time that you pulled me out of the ocean, my sister drowned.

ANTONIO It was a sad day!

SEBASTIAN People said that she looked like me, but she was beautiful. Although I could not believe that she looked like me, I still proclaimed her loveliness. She was fair-minded. She drowned in the sea, Antonio. I wash away memories of her with tears.

ANTONIO Please excuse the poor hospitality here.

SEBASTIAN Antonio, don't let me trouble you.

ANTONIO If you will not reject my offer, let me be your servant.

SEBASTIAN If you will not undo what you have done, that is, kill him whom you have recovered, desire it not. Fare ye well at once: my bosom is full of kindness, and I am yet so near the manners of my mother, that upon the least occasion more mine eyes will tell tales of me. I am bound to the Count Orsino's court. Farewell.
[Exit]

ANTONIO The gentleness of all the gods go with thee!
I have many enemies in Orsino's court,
Else would I very shortly see thee there.
But, come what may, I do adore thee so,
That danger shall seem sport, and I will go.
[Exit]

SEBASTIAN If you don't want to kill me, don't ask to be my servant. I must say good-bye immediately. My heart is touched by your kindness. I am so womanly that, like my mother, I will weep. I am going to the court of Count Orsino. Good-bye. *[SEBASTIAN departs.]*

ANTONIO God's grace go with you. If I didn't have enemies at Orsino's court, I would follow you. But, whatever happens to me, I am so fond of you that, even if danger awaits, I will come too. *[ANTONIO departs.]*

ACT II, SCENE 2

A street.

[Enter VIOLA, MALVOLIO following]

MALVOLIO Were not you even now with the Countess Olivia?

VIOLA Even now, sir; on a moderate pace I have since arrived but hither.

MALVOLIO She returns this ring to you, sir. You might have saved me my pains, to have taken it away yourself. She adds, moreover, that you should put your lord into a desperate assurance she will none of him; and one thing more, that you be never so hardy to come again in his affairs, unless it be to report your lord's taking of this. Receive it so.

VIOLA She took the ring of me; I'll none of it.

MALVOLIO Come, sir, you peevishly threw it to her; and her will is, it should be so returned. If it be worth stooping for, there it lies in your eye; if not, be it his that finds it. *[Exit]*

VIOLA
I left no ring with her. What means this lady?
Fortune forbid my outside have not charm'd her!
She made good view of me; indeed, so much
That sure methought her eyes had lost her tongue,
For she did speak in starts distractedly.
She loves me, sure; the cunning of her passion
Invites me in this churlish messenger.
None of my lord's ring! why, he sent her none.
I am the man. If it be so, as 'tis,
Poor lady, she were better love a dream.
Disguise, I see, thou art a wickedness,
Wherein the pregnant enemy does much.
How easy is it for the proper-false
In women's waxen hearts to set their forms!
Alas, our frailty is the cause, not we!
For such as we are made of, such we be.

ACT II, SCENE 2

A street in Illyria.

[VIOLA disguised as CESARIO enters the street. MALVOLIO follows her.]

MALVOLIO Did you just visit the Countess Olivia?

VIOLA Yes. I have walked at a slow pace from her residence.

MALVOLIO Sir, she gives you back this ring. You might have saved me the trouble and taken it with you. Olivia adds that you should assure Duke Orsino that she rejects him. Also, don't come back to the residence on his behalf unless you report the Duke's response to the return of the ring. Here it is.

VIOLA She accepted the ring. I won't take it back.

MALVOLIO Here, sir, is the ring you childishly tossed at her. She wants you to take it back. If it is worth bending over to pick up, you can see it here on the ground. If it is worthless, leave it here for somebody to find. *[MALVOLIO goes out.]*

VIOLA I didn't give her a ring. What does the Countess mean? Fate forbid that she was attracted to me in disguise! She looked me over. Her gaze seemed to silence her speech. She talked distractedly in fragments. Surely, she loves me. Her hidden emotion seeks the return of this boorish messenger boy. She rejects the Duke's ring? Why, he sent no ring. I am the man the Countess wants to see. If I am right, the poor Countess would be better off loving a fantasy. Wearing a disguise is sinful because it encourages Satan. It is so easy for a deceptive man to steal women's impressionable hearts! The fault is women's weakness, not the women themselves! We are as frail as our makeup.

How will this fadge? my master loves her dearly;
And I, poor monster, fond as much on him;
And she, mistaken, seems to dote on me.
What will become of this? As I am man,
My state is desperate for my master's love;
As I am woman,—now alas the day!
What thriftless sighs shall poor Olivia breathe!
O Time, thou must untangle this, not I!
It is too hard a knot for me to untie!
[Exit]

Out of error, the Countess adores me. How will this work out? Because I pose as a male, I can't win Duke Orsino's love. Because I am female, Olivia wastes her passion on me! Time must take care of this mix-up. I can't do it! It is too tight a knot for me to loosen! *[VIOLA disguised as CESARIO goes out.]*

ACT II, SCENE 3

Olivia's house.

[Enter SIR TOBY and SIR ANDREW]

SIR TOBY Approach, Sir Andrew. Not to be a-bed after midnight is to be up betimes; and 'diluculo surgere,' thou know'st.

SIR ANDREW Nay, by my troth, I know not; but I know, to be up late is to be up late.

SIR TOBY A false conclusion. I hate it as an unfilled can. To be up after midnight and to go to bed then, is early; so that to go to bed after midnight is to go to bed betimes. Does not our life consist of the four elements?

SIR ANDREW Faith, so they say; but I think it rather consists of eating and drinking.

SIR TOBY Thou'rt a scholar; let us therefore eat and drink. Marian, I say! a stoup of wine!
[Enter CLOWN]

SIR ANDREW Here comes the fool, i' faith.

CLOWN How now, my hearts! did you never see the picture of 'We Three'?

SIR TOBY Welcome, ass. Now let's have a catch.

SIR ANDREW By my troth, the fool has an excellent breast. I had rather than forty shillings I had such a leg, and so sweet a breath to sing, as the fool has. In sooth, thou wast in very gracious fooling last night, when thou spokest of Pigrogromitus, of the Vapians passing the equinoctial of Queubus. 'Twas very good, i' faith. I sent thee sixpence for thy leman. Hadst it?

CLOWN I did impeticos thy gratillity: for Malvolio's nose is no whipstock; my lady has a white hand, and the Myrmidons are no bottle-ale houses.

SIR ANDREW Excellent! why, this is the best fooling, when all is done. Now, a song.

SIR TOBY Come on; there is sixpence for you. Let's have a song.

ACT II, SCENE 3

The residence of the Countess Olivia.

[SIR TOBY and SIR ANDREW enter.]

SIR TOBY Come on, Sir Andrew. Staying up after midnight means we are up early. You know the old saying, "Excellent health comes from getting up early."

SIR ANDREW No, truly, I don't know that one. I do know that staying up late means we are up late.

SIR TOBY You analyze it improperly. I reject your conclusion as I reject an empty tankard. To stay up after midnight and to go to bed then means we were up early. To retire after midnight means to go to bed at the right time. Isn't the body made up of earth, air, fire, and water?

SIR ANDREW So they say. But I think the body comes from dining and drinking.

SIR TOBY You are brilliant. Then let us eat and drink. Maria, bring a pitcher of wine! *[FESTE the jester enters.]*

SIR ANDREW Here comes the jester.

CLOWN How is everyone? Have you seen the tavern sign of the three asses?

SIR TOBY You are welcome as the third ass. Let's sing a round.

SIR ANDREW Truly, Feste has an excellent voice. I would take his fine dancing rather than four dollars. I would have such sweet singing voice as Feste. You entertained us well last night. I liked the story of Pigrogromitus, the Vapian who spent the equinox at Queubus. That was a good story. I sent six pennies for your girlfriend. Did you get it?

CLOWN I pocketed your gift. Malvolio's long nose pokes into everything. My lady is a gentlewoman. The Myrmidon tavern we frequent serves better than bottled beer.

SIR ANDREW Excellent. I enjoy your sense of humor above all. Now, sing for us.

SIR TOBY Please do. Here are six pennies for you. Sing for us.

SIR ANDREW There's a testril of me too. If one knight give a—

CLOWN Would you have a love song, or a song of good life?

SIR TOBY A love song, a love song.

SIR ANDREW Ay, ay. I care not for good life.

CLOWN *[Sings.]* O mistress mine, where are you roaming?
O, stay and hear; your true love's coming,
That can sing both high and low.
Trip no further, pretty sweeting;
Journeys end in lovers meeting,
Every wise man's son doth know.

SIR ANDREW Excellent good, i' faith.

SIR TOBY Good, good.

CLOWN *[Sings.]* What is love? 'tis not hereafter;
Present mirth hath present laughter;
What's to come is still unsure.
In delay there lies no plenty;
Then come kiss me, sweet and twenty,
Youth's a stuff will not endure.

SIR ANDREW A mellifluous voice, as I am true knight.

SIR TOBY A contagious breath.

SIR ANDREW Very sweet and contagious, i' faith.

SIR TOBY To hear by the nose, it is dulcet in contagion.
But shall we make the welkin dance indeed?
Shall we rouse the night-owl in a catch that will draw three souls out of one weaver? Shall we do that?

SIR ANDREW An you love me, let's do't. I am dog at a catch.

CLOWN By'r lady, sir, and some dogs will catch well.

SIR ANDREW Most certain. Let our catch be, 'Thou knave.'

CLOWN 'Hold thy peace, thou knave,' knight? I shall be constrained in't to call thee knave, knight.

SIR ANDREW 'Tis not the first time I have constrained one to call me knave. Begin, fool. It begins 'Hold thy peace.'

SIR ANDREW I will give you a coin as well. If one horseman gives a—

CLOWN Do you want a love song or a moral song?

SIR TOBY A love song, a love song.

SIR ANDREW Yes, yes. I don't care for moral tunes.

CLOWN *[FESTE sings.]* Oh, my lady, where are you going? Stay here and listen. Your sweetheart is coming to sing high and low. Venture no farther, pretty sweetheart. Every wiseman's son knows that journeys are finished when lovers meet.

SIR ANDREW Well done.

SIR TOBY Good, good.

CLOWN *[FESTE sings.]* What is love? It does not exist after death. Fun in the real world gives immediate pleasure. The afterlife is uncertain. Waiting for joy leaves us unfilled. Kiss me, sweetheart, twenty times. We won't be young forever.

SIR ANDREW As I am a true horseman, Feste has a honeyed voice.

SIR TOBY That's a catchy tune.

SIR ANDREW Tuneful and memorable, I say.

SIR TOBY If the nose could hear, the song would smell sweet in dirty air. Shall we make the sky dance? Shall we awaken the night owl with a round that will draw three singers in tune with the one who begins the melody? Shall we sing together?

SIR ANDREW If you are my friend, let's sing together. I am as good at a round as a dog playing catch.

CLOWN By the Virgin Mary, sir, some dogs are expert at fetching.

SIR ANDREW They certainly are. Let's sing "You rascal."

CLOWN Do you mean "Be quiet, you rascal," Sir Andrew? The lyrics will make me call you a rogue, sir.

SIR ANDREW It won't be the first time that someone has called me a rogue. Start the tune, Feste. It begins, "Hush up."

CLOWN I shall never begin if I hold my peace.

SIR ANDREW Good, i' faith. Come, begin.
[Catch sung]
[Enter MARIA]

MARIA What a caterwauling do you keep here! If my lady
have not called up her steward Malvolio and
bid him turn you out of doors, never trust me.

SIR TOBY My lady's a Cataian, we are politicians, Malvolio's
a Peg-a-Ramsey, and 'Three merry men be we.'
Am not I consanguineous? am I not of her blood?
Tillyvally. Lady! *[Sings]* 'There dwelt a man in
Babylon, lady, lady!'

CLOWN Beshrew me, the knight's in admirable fooling.

SIR ANDREW Ay, he does well enough if he be disposed, and so do
I too. He does it with a better grace, but I do it more
natural.

SIR TOBY *[Sings]* 'Oh, the twelfth day of December.'

MARIA For the love o' God, peace!
[Enter MALVOLIO]

MALVOLIO My masters, are you mad? or what are you? Have you
no wit, manners, nor honesty, but to gabble like tinkers
at this time of night? Do ye make an ale-house of my
lady's house, that ye squeak out your coziers' catches
without any mitigation or remorse of voice? Is there no
respect of place, persons, nor time in you?

SIR TOBY We did keep time, sir, in our catches. Sneck up!

MALVOLIO Sir Toby, I must be round with you. My lady bade me
tell you, that, thought she harbours you as her kinsman,
she's nothing allied to your disorders. If you can separate
yourself and your misdemeanors, you are welcome to
the house; if not, an it would please you to take leave
of her, she is very willing to bid you farewell.

SIR TOBY *[Sings.]* 'Farewell, dear heart, since I must needs be gone.'

MARIA Nay, good Sir Toby.

CLOWN *[Sings.]* 'His eyes do show his days are almost done.'

MALVOLIO Is't even so?

CLOWN I can't begin if I have to be silent.

SIR ANDREW That's a good joke. Come on, start the song. *[FESTE, SIR ANDREW, and SIR TOBY sing the round.]* *[MARIA enters.]*

MARIA What a racket you make here! Trust me, the Countess Olivia will have her steward Malvolio throw you out.

SIR TOBY Olivia is a wily Chinese, we are schemers, Malvolio's a scoundrel, and the three of us are jolly. Aren't I her relative? Aren't I a member of her family? Twaddle, she's a fine lady! *[SIR TOBY sings.]* In Babylon, my lady, lived a man!

CLOWN Bless me, Sir Toby's in fine spirits.

SIR ANDREW He is fun when he's in the mood and so am I. Sir Toby is more graceful at it, but I'm a natural fool.

SIR TOBY *[SIR TOBY sings.]* Oh, the twelfth day of December.

MARIA For God's love, shut up! *[MALVOLIO enters.]*

MALVOLIO Gentlemen, are you crazy? Why all the noise? Have you no sense, courtesy, or respect but to warble like gypsies late at night? Have you turned the Countess Olivia's home into a barroom? Do you squeak out your cobblers' tunes without softening or restraining your voices? Have you no respect for this place, this household, nor the time of night?

SIR TOBY We did respect the time in our rhythms. Break his neck!

MALVOLIO Sir Toby, I must speak plainly. My lady asked me to tell you that, although you are relatives, she doesn't share your taste for carousing. If you give up drunken binges, you are welcome to stay here. If you don't improve and you want to move on, she is eager to say good-bye.

SIR TOBY *[SIR TOBY sings.]* Goodbye, my dear, for I must leave.

MARIA No, Sir Toby.

CLOWN *[FESTE sings.]* His eyes look like those of a dying man.

MALVOLIO Is this true?

SIR TOBY *[Sings.]* 'But I will never die.'

CLOWN Sir Toby, there you lie.

MALVOLIO This is much credit to you.

SIR TOBY *[Sings.]* 'Shall I bid him go?'

CLOWN *[Sings.]* 'What an if you do?'

SIR TOBY *[Sings.]* 'Shall I bid him go, and spare not?'

CLOWN *[Sings.]* 'Oh, no, no, no, no, you dare not!'

SIR TOBY Out o' tune, sir! ye lie. Art any more than a steward? Dost thou think, because thou art virtuous, there shall be no more cakes and ale?

CLOWN Yes, by St. Anne, and ginger shall be hot i' the mouth too.

SIR TOBY Th' art I' th' right. Go, sir rub your chain with crumbs. A stoup of wine, Maria!

MALVOLIO Mistress Mary, if you prized my lady's favour at anything more than contempt, you would not give means for this uncivil rule. She shall know of it, by this hand. *[Exit]*

MARIA Go shake your ears.

SIR ANDREW 'Twere as good a deed as to drink when a man's a-hungry, to challenge him the field, and then to break promise with him and make a fool of him.

SIR TOBY Do't, knight. I'll write thee a challenge; or I'll deliver thy indignation to him by word of mouth.

MARIA Sweet Sir Toby, be patient for to-night. Since the youth of the count's was to-day with my lady, she is much out of quiet. For Monsieur Malvolio, let me alone with him; if I do not gull him into a nayword, and make him a common recreation, do not think I have wit enough to lie straight in my bed. I know I can do it.

SIR TOBY Possess us, possess us; tell us something of him.

MARIA Marry, sir, sometimes he is a kind of puritan.

SIR ANDREW Oh, if I thought that, I'd beat him like a dog.

SIR TOBY What, for being a puritan? thy exquisite reason, dear knight.

SIR TOBY	*[SIR TOBY sings.]* But I will never die.
CLOWN	Sir Toby, that's a lie.
MALVOLIO	You have made the right choice.
SIR TOBY	*[SIR TOBY sings.]* Shall I order him out?
CLOWN	*[FESTE sings.]* What will happen if you do?
SIR TOBY	*[SIR TOBY sings.]* Shall I order him out in plain language?
CLOWN	*[FESTE sings.]* Oh, no, no, no, no, don't you dare!
SIR TOBY	You are out of tune, Malvolio! You are false. Are you just a butler? Do you think that, because you don't carouse, that you can stop other people from enjoying cake and ale?
CLOWN	Yes, by St. Anne, Jesus's grandmother, and we shall enjoy hot spice in our drink.
SIR TOBY	You are correct. Go drag your keychain through crumbs. Maria, bring a pitcher of wine!
MALVOLIO	Maria, if you respected the Countess, you wouldn't allow this rude behavior. I promise, I will tell her about it. *[MALVOLIO goes out.]*
MARIA	Go shake your ears like a donkey, Malvolio.
SIR ANDREW	I should drink when I'm hungry, challenge Malvolio to a duel, and then leave him standing and humiliate him.
SIR TOBY	Do it, Sir Andrew. I'll write the formal challenge to the duel. Or I will tell Malvolio directly of your impertinence.
MARIA	Sir Toby, don't do anything tonight. Since Duke Orsino sent Cesario here today, the Countess has been troubled. Let me deal with Malvolio. Let me trick him with a proverb. I will turn him into a laughingstock. I am smart enough to lie flat in bed. I know I can succeed.
SIR TOBY	Tell us, tell us. We want to know more about him.
MARIA	Well, sir, sometimes he is a strict moralist.
SIR ANDREW	Had I known that, I'd have whipped him like a dog.
SIR TOBY	You would lash him for being a prude? What is your precise reason, Sir Andrew?

SIR ANDREW I have no exquisite reason for't, but I have reason good enough.

MARIA The devil a puritan that he is, or anything constantly, but a time-pleaser; an affectioned ass, that cons state without book and utters it by great swarths: the best persuaded of himself, so crammed, as he thinks, with excellencies, that it is his grounds of faith that all that look on him love him; and on that vice in him will my revenge find notable cause to work.

SIR TOBY What wilt thou do?

MARIA I will drop in his way some obscure epistles of love, wherein, by the colour of his beard, the shape of his leg, the manner of his gait, the expressure of his eye, forehead, and complexion, he shall find himself most feelingly personated. I can write very like my lady your niece; on a forgotten matter we can hardly make distinction of our hands.

SIR TOBY Excellent! I smell a device.

SIR ANDREW I have't in my nose too.

SIR TOBY He shall think, by the letters that thou wilt drop, that they come from my niece, and that she's in love with him.

MARIA My purpose is, indeed, a horse of that colour.

SIR ANDREW And your horse now would make him an ass.

MARIA Ass, I doubt not.

SIR ANDREW Oh, 'twill be admirable!

MARIA Sport royal, I warrant you. I know my physic will work with him. I will plant you two, and let the fool make a third, where he shall find the letter. Observe his construction of it. For this night, to bed, and dream on the event. Farewell.
[Exit]

SIR TOBY Good night, Penthesilea.

SIR ANDREW Before me, she's a good wench.

SIR TOBY She's a beagle, true-bred, and one that adores me. What o' that?

SIR ANDREW I have no precise reason, but I have a good enough excuse.

MARIA Malvolio is a malicious puritan. He is inconsistent, a follower of the current religious fashion. He is a pompous twirp. He memorizes passages and recites them in large chunks. He is so stuffed with pretense that he believes everyone admires him. His egotism is a good place to aim my trickery.

SIR TOBY How will you deceive him?

MARIA I will leave anonymous love letters describing the color of his beard, the shape of his leg, his style of walking, the expression on his face. He will believe the letters describe him. I will imitate the handwriting of the Countess Olivia. Our writing styles look very similar.

SIR TOBY Wonderful! I smell a trick.

SIR ANDREW Me, too.

SIR TOBY Malvolio will think that the anonymous letters come from the Countess. He will believe that she loves him.

MARIA That's what I have in mind.

SIR ANDREW You want to ridicule him.

MARIA I will turn him into an ass.

SIR ANDREW Oh, what a great idea!

MARIA This is fun for a king, I guarantee. I know my cure will work on him. I will post you two along with Feste at the place where Malvolio will find the letter. Watch him read it. Tonight, go to bed and dream of the fun. Good-bye. *[MARIA goes out.]*

SIR TOBY Good night, Queen of the Amazons.

SIR ANDREW I declare, she's a nifty girl.

SIR TOBY She's sharp as a purebred beagle. And she loves me. What do you think of that?

SIR ANDREW I was adored once too.

SIR TOBY Let's to bed, knight. Thou hadst need send for more money.

SIR ANDREW If I cannot recover your niece, I am a foul way out.

SIR TOBY Send for money, knight. If thou hast her not i' the end, call me cut.

SIR ANDREW If I do not, never trust me, take it how you will.

SIR TOBY Come, come, I'll go burn some sack; 'tis too late to go to bed now. Come, knight; come, knight.
[Exeunt]

SIR ANDREW I was once adored.

SIR TOBY Let's halt for the night, Sir Andrew. You may need to send for more cash.

SIR ANDREW If I don't impress the Countess, I have wasted my money.

SIR TOBY Send for more cash, sir. If you don't win Olivia's love, you can call me a short-tailed horse.

SIR ANDREW If I lose her, never trust me again, however you think of me.

SIR TOBY Come with me. I will heat some yellow wine. It is too late to go to bed. Come, sir. *[SIR ANDREW and SIR TOBY go out.]*

ACT II, SCENE 4

The Duke's palace.

[Enter DUKE, VIOLA, CURIO, and Others]

DUKE Give me some music. Now, good-morrow, friends.
Now, good Cesario, but that piece of song,
That old and antique song we heard last night.
Methought it did relieve my passion much,
More than light airs and recollected terms
Of these most brisk and giddy-paced times.
Come, but one verse.

CURIO He is not here, so please your lordship, that should sing it.

DUKE Who was it?

CURIO Feste, the jester, my lord; a fool that the lady Olivia's father took much delight in. He is about the house.

DUKE Seek him out, and play the tune the while.
[Exit CURIO; Music plays]
Come hither, boy. If ever thou shalt love,
In the sweet pangs of it remember me;
For such as I am all true lovers are,
Unstaid and skittish in all motions else,
Save in the constant image of the creature
That is beloved. How dost thou like this tune?

VIOLA It gives a very echo to the seat
Where Love is throned.

DUKE Thou dost speak masterly.
My life upon't, young though thou art, thine eye
Hath stay'd upon some favour that it loves.
Hath it not, boy?

VIOLA A little, by your favour.

DUKE What kind of woman is't?

VIOLA Of your complexion.

DUKE She is not worth thee, then. What years, i' faith?

VIOLA About your years, my lord.

ACT II, SCENE 4

The palace of Duke Orsino in Illyria east of Italy.

[DUKE ORSINO, VIOLA disguised as CESARIO, CURIO, and others enter.]

DUKE I want music. Good morning, friends. Cesario, I want only that old-fashioned melody we heard last night. It revived my spirits. I like it better than ditties and imitative songs of these fast-paced, dizzying times. Please, sing a stanza.

CURIO The singer is not here, your lordship.

DUKE Who sang it?

CURIO Feste, the jester, sir. He was the entertainer whom Lady Olivia's father liked. Feste is in the house.

DUKE Go find him and play the melody while you look for him. *[CURIO goes out. Musicians play the melody.]* Come here, Cesario. If you ever fall in love, think of my suffering for Olivia. All lovers feel as I do. They are restless and nervous unless they are near their beloved. How do you like the melody?

VIOLA It echoes from the core of love.

DUKE You have a way with words. Even though you are young, you have looked at a sweetheart with affection. Haven't you, boy?

VIOLA A little, sir.

DUKE What does she look like?

VIOLA She has the same face as you.

DUKE You deserve better. How old is she?

VIOLA About your age, sir.

DUKE
Too old, by heaven. Let still the woman take
An elder than herself; so wears she to him,
So sways she level in her husband's heart.
For, boy, however we do praise ourselves,
Our fancies are more giddy and unfirm,
More longing, wavering, sooner lost and worn,
Than women's are.

VIOLA
I think it well, my lord.

DUKE
Then let thy love be younger than thyself
Or thy affection cannot hold the bent;
For women are as roses, whose fair flower
Being once display'd, doth fall that very hour.

VIOLA
And so they are. Alas, that they are so;
To die, even when they to perfection grow!
[Re-enter CURIO and CLOWN]

DUKE
O fellow, come, the song we had last night.
Mark it, Cesario, it is old and plain;
The spinsters and the knitters in the sun,
And the free maids that weave their thread with bones
Do use to chant it. It is silly sooth,
And dallies with the innocence of love,
Like the old age.

CLOWN
Are you ready, sir?

DUKE
Ay; prithee, sing. *[Music; Song]*

CLOWN
Come away, come away, death,
And in sad cypress let me be laid;
Fly away, fly away, breath;
I am slain by a fair cruel maid.
My shroud of white, stuck all with yew,
O prepare it!
My part of death, no one so true
Did share it.
Not a flower, not a flower sweet,
On my black coffin let there be strown;
Not a friend, not a friend greet
My poor corpse, where my bones shall be thrown.
A thousand thousand sighs to save,
Lay me, oh, where
Sad true lover never find my grave,
To weep there!

DUKE
There's for thy pains.

DUKE She is too old, by God. Women should love older men. She can mature into the kind of woman her husband likes and thus hold his affection. However much men praise themselves, they are unstable and less reliable than women.

VIOLA I agree, sir.

DUKE Then love a younger woman or your romance will be short. Women are like roses. Their blossoms, once opened, quickly fade.

VIOLA Yes, they do. I regret their brief glory. They begin to wilt at the height of perfection! *[CURIO and FESTE enter.]*

DUKE Oh, Feste, sing the song we heard last night. Notice, Cesario, that is a simple, old-style tune. Old maids, women knitting in the sun, and carefree girls weaving thread from bobbins sing this song. It is a sentimental truth based on innocent infatuation, a common theme long ago.

CLOWN Are you ready, sir?

DUKE Yes, please, sing it. *[FESTE sings to the music.]*

CLOWN Come, death, and bury me in a cypress box. Life, fly away. A heartless girl has killed me. Ready my white shroud and deck it with yew branches. I accept death more truly than anyone before me. Deck my black coffin with no sweet blossoms. Let no friend view my remains or see where my bones are tossed. Bury me where no true lover will find me and weep with thousands of sighs.

DUKE Here is money for your performance.

CLOWN No pains, sir; I take pleasure in singing, sir.

DUKE I'll pay thy pleasure then.

CLOWN Truly, sir, and pleasure will be paid, one time or another.

DUKE Give me now leave to leave thee.

CLOWN Now, the melancholy god protect thee; and the tailor make thy doublet of changeable taffeta, for thy mind is a very opal. I would have men of such constancy put to sea, that their business might be everything and their intent everywhere; for that's it that always makes a good voyage of nothing. Farewell.
[Exit]

DUKE Let all the rest give place.
[CURIO and Attendants retire.]
Once more, Cesario,
Get thee to yond same sovereign cruelty.
Tell her, my love, more noble than the world,
Prizes not quantity of dirty lands;
The parts that fortune hath bestow'd upon her,
Tell her, I hold as giddily as fortune;
But 'tis that miracle and queen of gems,
That nature pranks her in, attracts my soul.

VIOLA But if she cannot love you, sir?

DUKE I cannot be so answer'd.

VIOLA Sooth, but you must.
Say that some lady, as perhaps there is,
Hath for your love as great a pang of heart
As you have for Olivia. You cannot love her;
You tell her so; must she not then be answer'd?

DUKE There is no woman's sides
Can bide the beating of so strong a passion
As love doth give my heart; no woman's heart
So big, to hold so much. They lack retention.
Alas, their love may be called appetite,—
No motion of the liver, but the palate,—
That suffer surfeit, cloyment and revolt;
But mine is all as hungry as the sea,
And can digest as much. Make no compare
Between that love a woman can bear me
And that I owe Olivia.

CLOWN It was no trouble. I love to sing, sir.

DUKE Here is money for your enjoyment of music.

CLOWN Indeed, sir, joy repays me eventually.

DUKE Excuse me. I am leaving.

CLOWN Let a pensive god protect you. Let the tailor make a vest for you out of two-toned taffeta, for your spirit is as unstable as the color of an opal. I would send men like you to sea to travel everywhere and see everything. They enjoy sailing nowhere in particular. Good-bye. *[FESTE goes out.]*

DUKE Everyone is excused. *[CURIO and the servants go away.]* Again, Cesario, go to the cruel Countess. Tell her that my noble affection has no need of property. I have no interest in the estate that she has inherited. My soul yearns for her jewel-like self.

VIOLA What if she never accepts you, sir?

DUKE I can't accept refusal.

VIOLA Truly, you must accept it. Suppose there were a woman who yearned for you as much as you ache for Olivia. You don't love this woman. After you reject her, shouldn't she accept your answer?

DUKE No woman's chest can tolerate the passion of my beating heart. No woman's heart is big enough to contain that much affection. Women are too shallow. Women's love is an appetite—not from the heart, but from their taste buds, which are soon satisfied, overfilled, and nauseated. My affection is as ravenous as the ocean and can contain as much. Don't compare any woman's affection to my love for Olivia.

VIOLA Ay, but I know—

DUKE What dost thou know?

VIOLA Too well what love women to men may owe.
In faith, they are as true of heart as we.
My father had a daughter loved a man,
As it might be, perhaps, were I a woman.
I should your lordship.

DUKE And what's her history?

VIOLA A blank, my lord. She never told her love,
But let concealment, like a worm i' the bud,
Feed on her damask cheek. She pined in thought,
And with a green and yellow melancholy
She sat like patience on a monument,
Smiling at brief. Was not this love indeed?
We men may say more, swear more; but indeed
Our shows are more than will; for still we prove
Much in our vows, but little in our love.

DUKE But died thy sister of her love, my boy?

VIOLA I am all the daughters of my father's house,
And all the brothers too; and yet I know not.
Sir, shall I to this lady?

DUKE Ay, that's the theme.
To her in haste; give her this jewel; say,
My love can give no place, bide no denay.
[Exeunt]

VIOLA Yes, but I think—

DUKE What do you think?

VIOLA I understand how women love men. Women love as truly as men. My father had a daughter who loved a man. If I were a woman, I would love you the same way.

DUKE What happened to her?

VIOLA No one knows, sir. She hid her passion. The concealment, like a worm eating a bud, devoured her pink cheeks. She brooded over love. Patiently, she posed like a statue with a wretched sadness inside and a smile on the outside. Isn't that true love? We men may swear that we love more passionately. Our outward displays of affection are greater than our actual desire. We exhibit love in our pledges, but less so in our feelings.

DUKE Did your sister die of love, Cesario?

VIOLA I am the last child of the family. But I can't answer you. Sir, shall I go to the Countess Olivia?

DUKE Yes, that's my aim. Go quickly. Give her this gem. Tell her my love refuses to die. Accept no refusal. *[DUKE ORSINO and VIOLA disguised as CESARIO depart.]*

ACT II, SCENE 5

Olivia's garden.

[Enter SIR TOBY, SIR ANDREW, and FABIAN]

SIR TOBY Come thy ways, Signior Fabian.

FABIAN Nay, I'll come; if I lose a scruple of this sport, let me be boiled to death with melancholy.

SIR TOBY Wouldst thou not be glad to have the niggardly rascally sheep-biter come by some notable shame?

FABIAN I would exult, man. You know, he brought me out o' favour with my lady about a bear-baiting here.

SIR TOBY To anger him we'll have the bear again; and we will fool him black and blue. Shall we not, Sir Andrew?

SIR ANDREW An we do not, it is pity of our lives.
[Enter MARIA]

SIR TOBY Here comes the little villain. How now, my metal of India!

MARIA Get ye all three into the box-tree. Malvolio's coming down this walk. He has been yonder i' the sun practising behaviour to his own shadow this half-hour. Observe him, for the love of mockery; for I know this letter will make a contemplative idiot of him. Close, in the name of jesting! Lie thou there *[Throws down a letter]*; for here comes the trout that must be caught with tickling.
[Exit]
[Enter MALVOLIO]

MALVOLIO 'Tis but fortune; all is fortune. Maria once told me she did affect me; and I have heard herself come thus near, that should she fancy, it should be one of my complexion. Besides, she uses me with a more exalted respect than any one else that follows her. What should I think on't?

SIR TOBY Here's an overweening rogue!

FABIAN Oh, peace! Contemplation makes a rare turkey-cock of him. How he jets under his advanced plumes!

ACT II, SCENE 5

The Countess Olivia's garden.

[SIR TOBY, SIR ANDREW, and FABIAN enter.]

SIR TOBY Come with us, Fabian.

FABIAN Of course I'll come. If I miss a moment of this game, let me be boiled in sadness.

SIR TOBY Do you want to see this prudish, wicked sheep-biter ridiculed?

FABIAN I would love it, sir. He caused me to lose my lady's admiration at a bear-baiting, where dogs tormented the bear.

SIR TOBY To anger Malvolio, we will make him the bear. We will bruise him black and blue with tricks. Won't we, Sir Andrew?

SIR ANDREW If we don't, it would be a pity to miss this once-in-a-lifetime opportunity. *[MARIA enters.]*

SIR TOBY Here comes the little joker. Greetings, gold of India!

MARIA All three of you must hide in the boxwood hedge. Malvolio is walking this way. He has been standing in sunlight for thirty minutes practicing poses with his shadow. Watch him, for the sake of fun. I know this anonymous letter will make him fantasize like a fool. Stay down to observe the spectacle. I will put this here. *[MARIA tosses the anonymous letter on the path.]* Here comes a trout that we can catch by tickling him. *[MARIA goes out.]*
[MALVOLIO enters.]

MALVOLIO It's all a matter of luck, sheer luck. Maria once said she liked me. I have heard her come near to admitting that, if she loved any man, he would look like me. Also, she respects me more than anyone else I've met. How should I interpret that?

SIR TOBY Here's an arrogant twit!

FABIAN Hush! Imagination turns him into a swaggering turkey. How he struts beneath raised feathers!

SIR ANDREW 'Slight, I could so beat the rogue!

SIR TOBY Peace, I say.

MALVOLIO To be Count Malvolio!

SIR TOBY Ah, rogue!

SIR ANDREW Pistol him, pistol him.

SIR TOBY Peace, peace!

MALVOLIO There is example for't; the Lady of the Strachy married the yeoman of the wardrobe.

SIR ANDREW Fie on him, Jezebel!

FABIAN O, peace! now he's deeply in. Look how imagination blows him.

MALVOLIO Having been three months married to her, sitting in my state,—

SIR TOBY Oh, for a stone-bow, to hit him in the eye.

MALVOLIO Calling my officers about me, in my branched velvet gown; having come from a day-bed, where I have left Olivia sleeping,—

SIR TOBY Fire and brimstone!

FABIAN Oh, peace, peace!

MALVOLIO And then to have the humour of state; and after a demure travel of regard, telling them I know my place as I would they should do theirs, to ask for my kinsman Toby,—

SIR TOBY Bolts and shackles!

FABIAN Oh, peace, peace, peace! now, now.

MALVOLIO Seven of my people, with an obedient start, make out for him. I frown the while; and perchance wind up my watch, or play with my—some rich jewel. Toby approaches; courtesies there to me,—

SIR TOBY Shall this fellow live?

FABIAN Though our silence be drawn from us with cars, yet peace.

MALVOLIO I extend my hand to him thus, quenching my familiar smile with an austere regard of control,—

SIR ANDREW God's light, I would love to beat him up!

SIR TOBY Please, hush.

MALVOLIO I want to be Count Malvolio!

SIR TOBY Oh, scoundrel!

SIR ANDREW Pistol-whip him.

SIR TOBY Hush, hush!

MALVOLIO There have been other lowly men advanced in rank. The Lady Strachy married the wardrobe manager.

SIR ANDREW Shame on the yeoman, hussy!

FABIAN Be quiet! Now he's hooked. Look how fantasy overtakes him.

MALVOLIO I can see myself sitting in glory after three months of marriage to the Countess.

SIR TOBY I would love to aim a catapult at his eye.

MALVOLIO In a figured velvet robe, I would summon my officers. After coming from the lounge, where I left Olivia sleeping.

SIR TOBY Fire and sulfur!

FABIAN Oh, shut up!

MALVOLIO I would wear the dignity of a statesman. After surveying the group, I would tell them to remember their status as I would exhibit mine. I would call for my in-law, Uncle Toby.

SIR TOBY Bolts and chains!

FABIAN Oh, shut up now.

MALVOLIO Seven of my staff would obediently go find him. I would continue scowling. I might wind my watch. Or toy with my—with an expensive jewel. Sir Toby would enter. He would bow to me.

SIR TOBY Can I let him live?

FABIAN Even if we be tortured and ripped apart by chariots, be still.

MALVOLIO I would gesture to him, covering a smile with a somber expression—

SIR TOBY And does not Toby take you a blow o' the lips then?

MALVOLIO Saying, 'Cousin Toby, my fortunes having cast me on your niece give me this prerogative of speech.'

SIR TOBY What, what?

MALVOLIO 'You must amend your drunkenness.'

SIR TOBY Out, scab!

FABIAN Nay, patience, or we break the sinews of our plot.

MALVOLIO 'Besides, you waste the treasure of your time with a foolish knight'—

SIR ANDREW That's me, I warrant you.

MALVOLIO 'One Sir Andrew'—

SIR ANDREW I knew 'twas I; for many do call me fool.

MALVOLIO What employment have we here? *[Takes up the letter]*

FABIAN Now is the woodcock near the gin.

SIR TOBY Oh, peace! and the spirit of humours intimate reading aloud to him!

MALVOLIO By my life, this is my lady's hand. These be her very C's, her U's, and her T's; and thus makes she her great P's. It is, in contempt of question, her hand.

SIR ANDREW Her C's, her U's, and her T's. Why that?

MALVOLIO *[Reads]* 'To the unknown beloved, this, and my good wishes.' Her very phrases! By your leave, wax. Soft, and the impressure her Lucrece, with which she uses to seal. 'Tis my lady. To whom should this be?

FABIAN This wins him liver and all.

MALVOLIO *[Reads]*
Jove knows I love;
But who?
Lips, do not move;
No man must know.
'No man must know.' What follows? the numbers altered. 'No man must know.' If this should be thee, Malvolio?

SIR TOBY Marry, hang thee, brock!

SIR TOBY Then wouldn't I love to smack you in the mouth?

MALVOLIO I would say, "Kinsman Toby, the luck that made me husband of your niece allows me to speak openly to you."

SIR TOBY How dare he!

MALVOLIO "You must stop carousing."

SIR TOBY Out, scab!

FABIAN Be quiet or we will destroy the game.

MALVOLIO "You waste your time with a foolish companion."

SIR ANDREW He refers to me, I guarantee.

MALVOLIO "With Sir Andrew—"

SIR ANDREW I knew it. Lots of people call me a dolt.

MALVOLIO What communication is this letter? *[MALVOLIO picks up the anonymous letter.]*

FABIAN The snipe is approaching the trap.

SIR TOBY Oh, be silent. The power of comedy communicates with him.

MALVOLIO I declare, this is the Countess Olivia's handwriting. The C, U, and T look like her style. This the way she shapes a capital P. Unquestionably, this is her handwriting.

SIR ANDREW Why does he mention C, U, and T?

MALVOLIO *[MALVOLIO reads aloud.]* "To the man I love in secret, I address this letter and my greeting." Those are words that she often speaks! With your permission, I will break the wax seal. Still soft and engraved with the likeness of Lucretia, the Roman noblewoman, whom the Countess uses on her carved seal. The Countess wrote this letter. To whom did she intend to send it?

FABIAN We've got him in our trap, up to the liver.

MALVOLIO *[MALVOLIO reads the letter.]* Jupiter knows that I love.
But whom do I love? Lips, say nothing. No one must
know. What comes next? The rhythm changes.
"No one must know." Could she mean you, Malvolio?

SIR TOBY Indeed, hang you, skunk!

MALVOLIO *[Reads]*
I may command where I adore;
But silence, like a Lucrece knife,
With bloodless stroke my heart doth gore.
M, O, A, I, doth sway my life.

FABIAN A fustian riddle!

SIR TOBY Excellent wench, say I.

MALVOLIO 'M, O, A, I, doth sway my life.' Nay, but first, let me see, let me see, let me see.

FABIAN What dish o' poison has she dressed him?

SIR TOBY And with what wing the staniel checks at it!

MALVOLIO 'I may command where I adore.' Why she may command me: I serve her; she is my lady. Why, this is evident to any formal capacity; there is no obstruction in this. And the end,—what should that alphabetical position portend? If I could make that resemble something in me! Softly! 'M, O, A, I.'

SIR TOBY Oh, ay, make up that; he is now at a cold scent.

FABIAN Sowter will cry upon't for all this, though it be as rank as a fox.

MALVOLIO M,—Malvolio; M,—why, that begins my name.

FABIAN Did not I say he would work it out? the cur is excellent at faults.

MALVOLIO M,—but then there is no consonancy in the sequel; that suffers under probation. A should follow, but O does.

FABIAN And O shall end, I hope.

SIR TOBY Ay or I'll cudgel him, and make him cry O!

MALVOLIO And then I comes behind.

FABIAN Ay, an you had any eye behind you, you might see more detraction at your heels than fortunes before you.

MALVOLIO *[MALVOLIO continues reading the anonymous letter.]* "I may give you orders, but actually I adore you. But secrecy, like the knife that Lucretia used to kill herself, pierces my heart without shedding blood. Ruling my life is MOAI."

FABIAN A ridiculous puzzle!

SIR TOBY Maria did a good job, I think.

MALVOLIO "Ruling my life is MOAI." Well, let me think on this.

FABIAN Maria has prepared him a poisoned dish!

SIR TOBY How eagerly the hawk pursues a worthless bird!

MALVOLIO "I may give you orders, but actually I adore you." She is my mistress. I serve her as a member of her staff. This is obvious to my mind. There is no problem in understanding this line. And the conclusion. . . . What do those letters mean? Could I make them refer to me? Wait! "MOAI. . . ."

SIR TOBY Oh, yes, make up something. He follows a cold trail.

FABIAN A bloodhound would bay at this clue, if it were as smelly as a fox.

MALVOLIO *M* stands for Malvolio. The *M* refers to me.

FABIAN Didn't I predict that he would figure it out? This stray dog is excellent at making errors.

MALVOLIO *M*—but I can't figure out the next letter. It does not make sense. An *A* should follow the *M* instead of an *O*.

FABIAN The word should end in *O*.

SIR TOBY Yes, or I'll smack him, and make him cry *O*!

MALVOLIO Then *I* comes next.

FABIAN Yes. If you had vision, you would see more trickery than good luck in front of you.

MALVOLIO M, O, A, I. This simulation is not as the former; and yet, to crush this a little, it would bow to me, for every one of these letters are in my name. Soft! here follows prose.

[Reads] 'If this fall into thy hand, revolve. In my stars I am above thee; but be not afraid of greatness. Some are born great, some achieve greatness, and some have greatness thrust upon 'em. Thy fates open their hands; let thy blood and spirit embrace them; and, to inure thyself to what thou art like to be, cast thy humble slough and appear fresh. Be opposite with a kinsman, surly with servants; let thy tongue tang arguments of state; put thyself into the trick of singularity. She thus advises thee that sighs for thee. Remember who commended thy yellow stockings, and wished to see thee ever cross-gartered. I say, remember. Go to, thou art made, if thou desirest to be so; if not, let me see thee a steward still, the fellow of servants, and not worthy to touch Fortune's fingers. Farewell. She that would alter services with thee,

The Fortunate Unhappy.'

Daylight and champian discovers not more. This is open. I will be proud, I will read politic authors, I will baffle Sir Toby, I will wash off gross acquaintance, I will be point-devise the very man. I do not now fool myself, to let imagination jade me; for every reason excites to this, that my lady loves me. She did commend my yellow stockings of late, she did praise my leg being cross-gartered; and in this she manifests herself to my love, and with a kind of injunction drives me to these habits of her liking. I thank my stars I am happy. I will be strange, stout, in yellow stockings, and cross-gartered, even with the swiftness of putting on. Jove and my stars be praised! Here is yet a postscript.

[Reads] 'Thou canst not choose but know who I am. If thou entertainest my love, let it appear in thy smiling. Thy smiles become thee well; therefore in my presence still smile, dear my sweet, I prithee.'

Jove, I thank thee. I will smile; I will do everything that thou wilt have me.

[Exit]

MALVOLIO *MOAI.* This is written differently. If I maneuver this a bit, the letters all appear in my name. Wait! There is a statement after the poem.
[MALVOLIO reads aloud from the anonymous letter.] "If you should find this letter, ponder it. In status, I am higher than you. Don't fear my rank. Some people are great at birth. Some make themselves great. Some find advancement by accident. Your destiny is generous. Let your whole being accept good fortune. To learn to be great, give up your lowly state and start over as a nobleman. Quarrel with relatives, grumble at servants. Venture into political discussions. Think like an individual. This is advice from a woman who yearns for you. Think of me as the person who liked you in yellow hose and who wanted to see you tie your garters around your knee in a bow. Remember this. If you like this proposition, then accept it. If not, stay a steward, an equal of servants. And don't reach out toward good luck. Good-bye. I am a woman who would make you my master. –A lucky, but unhappy woman."

Daylight and open ground are no clearer than this letter. It is obvious. I will be dignified. I will read learned writers. I will puzzle Sir Toby with my learning. I will rid myself of lowly friends. I will be the perfect gentleman. I am not imagining this. Fantasy is not tricking me. Every clue indicates that the Countess Olivia loves me. She did admire my yellow hose recently. She liked my garters tied around my knee in a bow. In these comments, she reveals affection for me. Because of her remarks, I dress as she likes. I thank good fortune for making me happy. I will stand arrogantly apart in yellow hose with my garters tied in bows at my knee as soon as I can put them on. Jupiter and my horoscope be thanked! Here is an addition to the letter. *[MALVOLIO reads aloud from the anonymous letter.]* "You must wonder who I am. If you love me too, then smile at me. You look handsome when you smile. Whenever I am near you, please smile, my sweetheart."

Thanks to Jupiter, I will smile at you. I will do whatever you want. *[MALVOLIO goes out.]*

FABIAN I will not give my part of this sport for a pension of thousands to be paid from the Sophy.

SIR TOBY I could marry this wench for this device.

SIR ANDREW So could I too.

SIR TOBY And ask no other dowry with her but such another jest.

SIR ANDREW Nor I neither.

FABIAN Here comes my noble gull-catcher.
[Re-enter MARIA]

SIR TOBY Wilt thou set thy foot o' my neck?

SIR ANDREW Or o' mine either?

SIR TOBY Shall I play my freedom at tray-trip, and become thy bond-slave?

SIR ANDREW I' faith, or I either?

SIR TOBY Why, thou hast put him in such a dream, that when the image of it leaves him he must run mad.

MARIA Nay, but say true; does it work upon him?

SIR TOBY Like aqua vitae with a midwife.

MARIA If you will then see the fruits of the sport, mark his first approach before my lady. He will come to her in yellow stockings, and 'tis a colour she abhors; and cross-gartered, a fashion she detests; and he will smile upon her, which will now be so unsuitable to her disposition, being addicted to a melancholy as she is, that it cannot but turn him into a notable contempt. If you will see it, follow me.

SIR TOBY To the gates of Tartar, thou most excellent devil of wit!

SIR ANDREW I'll make one too.
[Exeunt]

FABIAN I would not give up this joke for a pension of thousands paid from the Persian treasury.

SIR TOBY I would marry Maria for making up this plot.

SIR ANDREW So would I.

SIR TOBY I would seek no more dowry than another trick on Malvolio.

SIR ANDREW Me too.

FABIAN Here does the great catcher of fools. *[MARIA returns.]*

SIR TOBY Will the victor put her foot on her opponent's neck?

SIR ANDREW Or on mine?

SIR TOBY Shall I risk my freedom on a dice game and become your slave?

SIR ANDREW Or me?

SIR TOBY You have so filled him with fantasies that he will go mad when he realizes the truth.

MARIA Tell me, did he fall for it?

SIR TOBY Like a midwife drinking a stimulant.

MARIA If you want to see the results, watch him when he appears before the Countess. He will wear yellow hose, a color she hates. He will tie his garters at the knee in a bow, a style she loathes. He will smile at her. The smile will annoy her sad mood. She will despise him. If you want to watch, come along with me.

SIR TOBY I would follow you to the gates of hell, you witty demon!

SIR ANDREW Me too. *[FABIAN, MARIA, SIR ANDREW, and SIR TOBY go out.]*

ACT III, SCENE 1

Olivia's garden.

[Enter VIOLA, and Clown with a tabor]

VIOLA Save thee, friend, and thy music. Dost thou live by thy tabor?

CLOWN No, sir, I live by the church.

VIOLA Art thou a churchman?

CLOWN No such matter, sir. I do live by the church; for I do live at my house, and my house doth stand by the church.

VIOLA So thou mayst say, the king lies by a beggar, if a beggar dwell near him; or, the church stands by thy tabor, if thy tabor stand by the church.

CLOWN You have said, sir. To see this age! A sentence is but a cheveril glove to a good wit. How quickly the wrong side may be turned outward!

VIOLA Nay, that's certain. They that dally nicely with words may quickly make them wanton.

CLOWN I would, therefore, my sister had had no name, sir.

VIOLA Why, man?

CLOWN Why, sir, her name's a word; and to dally with that word might make my sister wanton. But indeed words are very rascals since bonds disgraced them.

VIOLA Thy reason, man?

CLOWN Troth, sir, I can yield you none without words; and words are grown so false, I am loath to prove reason with them.

VIOLA I warrant thou art a merry fellow and carest for nothing.

CLOWN Not so, sir, I do care for something; but in my conscience, sir, I do not care for you. If that be to care for nothing, sir, I would it would make you invisible.

VIOLA Art not thou the Lady Olivia's fool?

ACT III, SCENE 1

The Countess Olivia's garden.

[VIOLA disguised as CESARIO enters and meets FESTE, who carries a small drum.]

VIOLA God save you, Feste, and your music. Do you earn a living by playing the drum?

CLOWN No, sir, I live by the church.

VIOLA Are you a minister?

CLOWN Not at all, sir. I live by the church. I live in my house, which stands beside the church.

VIOLA In similar fashion, you might say that a king lives alongside a pauper if the pauper resides near the king. Or that the church stands by your drum if your drum stands alongside the church.

CLOWN You speak the truth, sir. What a great time to be alive! A statement is like a kidskin glove to a sense of humor. The faulty side is easily flipped over.

VIOLA That's for sure. People who turn statements into dirty words quickly make them vulgar.

CLOWN I wish my sister were nameless, Sir.

VIOLA Why do you say that?

CLOWN Her name is only a word. To twist the word would make her indecent. Words are suspect now that people demand a bond in place of a verbal pledge.

VIOLA Why do you say that, Feste?

CLOWN I can give you no answer without words. Words have become so untrustworthy that I don't dare justify my reason in words.

VIOLA You are certainly jolly and carefree.

CLOWN No, I do worry about something. My conscience tells me not to care for you. If I cared for nothing, you would be invisible.

VIOLA Are you the Countess Olivia's jester?

CLOWN No, indeed, sir; the Lady Olivia has no folly. She will keep no fool, sir, till she be married; and fools are as like husbands as pilchards are to herrings; the husband's the bigger. I am indeed not her fool, but her corrupter of words.

VIOLA I saw thee late at the Count Orsino's.

CLOWN Foolery, sir, does walk about the orb like the sun, it shines everywhere. I would be sorry, sir, but the fool should be as oft with your master as with my mistress. I think I saw your wisdom there.

VIOLA Nay, an thou pass upon me, I'll no more with thee. Hold, there's expenses for thee.

CLOWN Now, Jove, in his next commodity of hair send thee a beard!

VIOLA By my troth, I'll tell thee, I am almost sick for one—*[aside]* though I would not have it grow on my chin. Is thy lady within?

CLOWN My lady is within, sir. I will construe to them whence you come. Who you are and what you would are out of my welkin, I might say element, but the word is overworn.
[Exit]

VIOLA This fellow is wise enough to play the fool;
And to do that well craves a kind of wit.
He must observe their mood on whom he jests,
The quality of persons, and the time,
And, like the haggard, check at every feather
That comes before his eye. This is a practice
As full of labour as a wise man's art;
For folly that he wisely shows is fit,
But wise men, folly-fall'n, quite taint their wit.
[Enter SIR TOBY and SIR ANDREW]

SIR TOBY Save you, gentlemen.

VIOLA And you, sir.

SIR ANDREW Dieu vous garde, monsieur.

VIOLA Et vous aussi; votre serviteur.

SIR ANDREW I hope, sir, you are; and I am yours.

CLOWN No, sir. The Countess isn't playful. She will tolerate no fool until she marries. Fools resemble husbands as minnows look like herrings. The husband is the bigger fool. I am not her jester, but a twister of words.

VIOLA Recently, I saw you with Count Orsino.

CLOWN Nonsense, sir, moves around the globe like the sun, shining on everything. You may regret that the jester visits Duke Orsino as much as he visits the Countess Olivia. I saw you at Duke Orsino's house.

VIOLA Before you make more fun of me, I will leave you. Here are coins for you.

CLOWN When God passes out hair, I hope he gives you a beard.

VIOLA I confide to you that I am lovesick for a man. *[VIOLA in private]* But I don't want hair on my chin. Is the Countess at home?

CLOWN The Countess is at home, sir. I will tell the family that you are here. Who you are and what you want are unknown to me. I could say "element" for "welkin," but "element" is overused. *[FESTE goes into the house.]*

VIOLA Feste is clever enough to be a jester. Clowning requires intelligence. He must analyze the mood of his audience. He must evaluate social status and the time of day. Like a hawk, he must study every feather that he sees. Making jokes is as demanding as the intellectual's work. The foolery that the jester performs earns him a living. When intellectuals attempt the same type of comedy, they discredit their intelligence. *[SIR TOBY and SIR ANDREW enter.]*

SIR TOBY God save you, gentlemen.

VIOLA And you, sir.

SIR ANDREW God protect you, sir.

VIOLA And you also. I am your servant.

SIR ANDREW I hope you are, sir. And I am yours.

SIR TOBY Will you encounter the house? my niece is desirous you should enter, if your trade be to her.

VIOLA I am bound to your niece, sir; I mean, she is the list of my voyage.

SIR TOBY Taste your legs, sir; put them to motion.

VIOLA My legs do better understand me, Sir, than I understand what you mean by bidding me taste my legs.

SIR TOBY I mean, to go, sir, to enter.

VIOLA I will answer you with gait and entrance. But we are prevented. *[Enter OLIVIA and MARIA]* Most excellent accomplished lady, the heavens rain odours on you!

SIR ANDREW That youth's a rare courtier. 'Rain odours,' well.

VIOLA My matter hath no voice, lady, but to your own most pregnant and vouchsafed ear.

SIR ANDREW 'Odours,' 'pregnant,' and 'vouchsafed.' I'll get 'em all three all ready.

OLIVIA Let the garden door be shut, and leave me to my hearing. *[Exeunt SIR TOBY, SIR ANDREW, and MARIA]* Give me your hand, sir.

VIOLA My duty, madam, and most humble service.

OLIVIA What is your name?

VIOLA Cesario is your servant's name, fair princess.

OLIVIA My servant, sir! 'Twas never merry world
Since lowly feigning was called compliment.
You're servant to the Count Orsino, youth.

VIOLA And he is yours, and his must needs be yours.
Your servant's servant is your servant, madam.

OLIVIA For him, I think not on him; for his thoughts,
Would they were blanks, rather than fill'd with me!

VIOLA Madam, I come to whet your gentle thoughts
On his behalf.

SIR TOBY	Won't you come in? My niece Olivia desires your company, if you came to see her.
VIOLA	I must see your niece, sir. She is the goal of my visit.
SIR TOBY	Test your legs, sir. Move on.
VIOLA	My legs will know what you want me to do, sir, if you explain what you mean by "taste."
SIR TOBY	I mean go, sir, enter the house.
VIOLA	I will reply with a step and entrance to the house. But someone is coming. *[OLIVA and MARIA meet them at the entrance.]* Most excellent and talented Countess, may God rain blessing on you!
SIR ANDREW	Cesario is an unusually skillful courtier. "Rain blessings," well said.
VIOLA	My matter is private, Countess, for only your receptive and eager ear.
SIR ANDREW	Cesario said "odors," "pregnant," and "vouchsafed." I will memorize all three words to use in my own speech.
OLIVIA	Shut the garden gate and leave me in private. *[SIR TOBY, SIR ANDREW, and MARIA depart.]* Give me your hand, sir.
VIOLA	I promise my duty, madam, and my humble service.
OLIVIA	What is your name?
VIOLA	My name is Cesario, lovely princess.
OLIVIA	You are my servant, sir? The world has been less happy since people began disguising their words with false compliments. Boy, you serve Duke Orsino.
VIOLA	He is your servant and must be your love. I, as Duke Orsino's servant, am your servant, ma'am.
OLIVIA	As for the Duke, I don't think about him. I wish he thought about nothing rather than to obsess over me!
VIOLA	Madam, I am here to turn your attention to him.

OLIVIA Oh, by your leave, I pray you,
I bade you never speak again of him;
But, would you undertake another suit,
I had rather hear you to solicit that
Than music from the spheres.

VIOLA Dear lady,—

OLIVIA Give me leave, beseech you. I did send,
After the last enchantment you did here,
A ring in chase of you; so did I abuse
Myself, my servant, and I fear me, you.
Under your hard construction must I sit,
To force that on you, in a shameful cunning,
Which you knew none of yours. What might you think?
Have you not set mine honour at the stake
And baited it with all the unmuzzled thoughts
That tyrannous heart can think? To one of your receiving
Enough is shown. A cypress, not a bosom,
Hideth my heart. So, let me hear you speak.

VIOLA I pity you.

OLIVIA That's a degree to love.

VIOLA No, not a grize; for 'tis a vulgar proof,
That very oft we pity enemies.

OLIVIA Why, then, methinks 'tis time to smile again.
O world, how apt the poor are to be proud!
If one should be a prey, how much the better
To fall before the lion than the wolf!
[Clock strikes]
The clock upbraids me with the waste of time.
Be not afraid, good youth, I will not have you;
And yet, when wit and youth is come to harvest,
Your wife is like to reap a proper man.
There lies your way, due west.

VIOLA Then westward-ho!
Grace and good disposition attend your ladyship!
You'll nothing, madam, to my lord by me?

OLIVIA Stay.
I prithee, tell me what thou think'st of me.

VIOLA That you do think you are not what you are.

OLIVIA If you please, don't mention him any more. If you discuss something else, I would rather hear you speak than to hear heavenly music.

VIOLA Dear lady . . .

OLIVIA Let me beg you. When you last left here, I sent a ring to you. I dishonored myself, my servant Malvolio, and you with the ring. I suffer your poor opinion of me for sneakily giving you a ring that you knew was not yours. What did you think about it? Have you tied my honor to a stake and tormented it with fierce thoughts from an angry heart? To a person as sensitive as you, the ring trick was obvious. A thin veil, not flesh, covers my heart. Tell me what you think.

VIOLA I am sorry for you.

OLIVIA Pity is a kind of affection.

VIOLA No, not even a shadow of love. It is not uncommon to pity an enemy.

OLIVIA You give me reason to smile. Oh, the poor have reason to be proud! It is more prestigious to be stalked by the lion Orsino than by the wolf Cesario! *[OLIVIA's clock strikes.]* The clock reminds me not to waste time. Don't worry, Cesario, I will not court you. I admit that, when a woman harvests your intelligence and youth, she will gain a worthy mate. Leave and travel west.

VIOLA I will go west. I wish God's grace and contentment to you, Countess. You have no message for me to take back to Duke Orsino?

OLIVIA Don't go. Please, what is your opinion of me?

VIOLA That you encourage false impressions.

OLIVIA If I think so, I think the same of you.

VIOLA Then think you right; I am not what I am.

OLIVIA I would you were as I would have you be!

VIOLA Would it be better, madam, than I am?
I wish it might, for now I am your fool.

OLIVIA Oh, what a deal of scorn looks beautiful
In the contempt and anger of his lip!
A murderous guilt shows not itself more soon
Than love that would seem hid. Love's night is noon.
Cesario, by the roses of the spring,
By maidhood, honour, truth and everything,
I love thee so, that, maugre all thy pride,
Nor wit nor reason can my passion hide.
Do not extort thy reasons from this clause,
For that I woo, thou therefore hast no cause;
But rather reason thus with reason fetter,
Love sought is good, but given unsought is better.

VIOLA By innocence I swear, and by my youth,
I have one heart, one bosom and one truth,
And that no woman has; nor never none
Shall mistress be of it, save I alone.
And so adieu, good madam. Never more
Will I my master's tears to you deplore.

OLIVIA Yet come again; for thou perhaps mayest move
That heart, which now abhors, to like his love.
[Exeunt]

OLIVIA So, you do the same.

VIOLA You are correct. I am not what I appear to be.

OLIVIA I wish you were what I want you to be!

VIOLA Would you be happier if you could remake me? I wish you success, for now I am your jester.

OLIVIA Even your angry and scornful expression seems beautiful. It is easier to conceal guilt for murder than to hide affection. Even in the dark, love shines brightly. Cesario, by roses that bloom in spring, I love you with my virginity, prestige, truth, and everything I have. Even though you are too proud, my intelligence and sanity cannot conceal my passion. Don't think up reasons to dispute me. You have no reason to reply to my courtship. Match this logic with logic. Love that you pursue is good. Love that comes unbidden is better.

VIOLA I vow by my innocence and youth that I have a heart and awareness unlike that of any woman. No woman shall control my heart except me alone. And so, God be with you, madam. I will never bother you again with Duke Orsino's passion.

OLIVIA Please return again. Perhaps you can persuade me to love him. *[CESARIO and the COUNTESS OLIVIA depart.]*

ACT III, SCENE 2

A room in Olivia's house.

[Enter SIR TOBY, SIR ANDREW, and FABIAN]

SIR ANDREW No, faith, I'll not stay a jot longer.

SIR TOBY Thy reason, dear venom, give thy reason.

FABIAN You must needs yield your reason, Sir Andrew.

SIR ANDREW Marry, I saw your niece do more favours to the count's serving-man than ever she bestowed upon me. I saw't i' the orchard.

SIR TOBY Did she see thee the while, old boy? Tell me that.

SIR ANDREW As plain as I see you now.

FABIAN This was a great argument of love in her toward you.

SIR ANDREW Will you make an ass o' me?

FABIAN I will prove it legitimate, sir, upon the oaths of judgment and reason.

SIR TOBY And they have been grand-jurymen since before Noah was a sailor.

FABIAN She did show favour to the youth in your sight only to exasperate you, to awake your dormouse valour, to put fire in your heart, and brimstone in your liver. You should then have accosted her; and with some excellent jests, fire-new from the mint, you should have hanged the youth into dumbness. This was looked for at your hand, and this was balked. The double gilt of this opportunity you let time wash off, and you are now sailed into the north of my lady's opinion, where you will hang like an icicle on a Dutchman's beard, unless you do redeem it by some laudable attempt either of valour or policy.

SIR ANDREW An't be any way, it must be with valour; for policy I hate. I had as lief be a Brownist as a politician.

ACT III, SCENE 2

A room in the residence of the Countess Olivia in Illyria east of Italy.

[SIR TOBY, SIR ANDREW, and FABIAN enter.]

SIR ANDREW I won't stay another minute.

SIR TOBY What is your reason, dear serpent?

FABIAN You have to give us a reason, Sir Andrew.

SIR ANDREW I watched your niece be more polite to Duke Orsino's servant than she ever was to me. I watched in the orchard.

SIR TOBY Did she notice you, old boy? Tell me about it.

SIR ANDREW As clearly as I see you now.

FABIAN She has a good reason to love you.

SIR ANDREW Are you mocking me?

FABIAN I will prove it, sir, with judgment and logic.

SIR TOBY There have been great pleaders of cases since before Noah sailed on the ark.

FABIAN She flirted with Cesario in your sight alone to annoy you. She wanted to spur your courage, to put passion in your heart, to fire up your liver. You should confront her. With witty remarks, newly minted, you should have silenced Cesario. Olivia expected your retort. You passed up your chance. You wasted a golden opportunity and you have fallen into her disfavor. You will dangle like an icicle on a Dutchman's beard unless you redeem yourself with some proof of courage or strategy.

SIR ANDREW I will have to do it with courage. I hate strategy. I would rather be a religious fanatic than a politician.

SIR TOBY Why then, build me thy fortunes upon the basis of valour. Challenge me the count's youth to fight with him; hurt him in eleven places. My niece shall take note of it; and assure thyself, there is no love-broker in the world can more prevail in man's commendation with woman than report of valour.

FABIAN There is no way but this, Sir Andrew.

SIR ANDREW Will either of you bear me a challenge to him?

SIR TOBY Go, write it in a martial hand; be curst and brief; it is no matter how witty, so it be eloquent and full of invention. Taunt him with the licence of ink. If thou thou'st him some thrice, it shall not be amiss; and as many lies as will lie in thy sheet of paper, although the sheet were big enough for the bed of Ware in England, set 'em down. Go, about it. Let there be gall enough in thy ink; though thou write with a goose-pen, no matter. About it.

SIR ANDREW Where shall I find you?

SIR TOBY We'll call thee at the cubiculo. Go.
[Exit SIR ANDREW]

FABIAN This is a dear manakin to you, Sir Toby.

SIR TOBY I have been dear to him, lad, some two thousand strong, or so.

FABIAN We shall have a rare letter from him; but you'll not deliver't?

SIR TOBY Never trust me, then; and by all means stir on the youth to an answer. I think oxen and wainropes cannot hale them together. For Andrew, if he were opened, and you find so much blood in his liver as will clog the foot of a flea, I'll eat the rest of the anatomy.

FABIAN And his opposite, the youth, bears in his visage no great presage of cruelty.
[Enter MARIA]

SIR TOBY Look, where the youngest wren of nine comes.

SIR TOBY Why, risk your luck on courage. Challenge Cesario to a fight. Wound him eleven times. My niece will take an interest. No matchmaker in the world can so raise a man's worth with a woman than with a good fight.

FABIAN This is the only way, Sir Andrew.

SIR ANDREW Will one of you take my formal challenge to Cesario?

SIR TOBY Go and compose it in a warlike script. Be evil-tempered and curt. Don't make it funny. Be eloquent and imaginative. Sneer at him in print. If you honor him as "thou" three times, you will annoy him. And even if the stationery is as wide as a bed for twelve, fill it with lies. Get to it. Use bitter ink. Even though you write with a goose quill, it doesn't matter. Write it.

SIR ANDREW Where will I rejoin you?

SIR TOBY We will come for you in your little room. Go. *[SIR ANDREW goes out.]*

FABIAN You handle Sir Andrew like a puppet, Sir Toby.

SIR TOBY I have been an expensive puppeteer to him, Fabian, to the amount of two thousand or more.

FABIAN He will write an unusual letter. Will you deliver it?

SIR TOBY Certainly. Incite Cesario to a reply by any means. Oxen and wagon ropes can't haul them together. If you look in Andrew's liver and find as much blood as would fill a flea's foot, I'll eat the rest of the carcass.

FABIAN The expression of Cesario, his adversary, looks fierce. *[MARIA enters.]*

SIR TOBY Look at the smallest wren.

MARIA If you desire the spleen, and will laugh yourselves into stitches, follow me. Yond gull Malvolio is turned heathen, a very renegado; for there is no Christian, that means to be saved by believing rightly, can ever believe such impossible passages of grossness. He's in yellow stockings.

SIR TOBY And cross-gartered?

MARIA Most villainously, like a pedant that keeps a school i' the church. I have dogged him, like his murderer. He does obey every point of the letter that I dropped to betray him. He does smile his face into more lines than is in the new map with the augmentation of the Indies; you have not seen such a thing as 'tis. I can hardly forbear hurling things at him. I know my lady will strike him. If she do, he'll smile and take't for a great favour.

SIR TOBY Come, bring us, bring us where he is.
[Exeunt]

MARIA If you want revenge and to laugh yourself into stitches, follow me. That idiot Malvolio has turned into a savage, a real desperado. There is no believer of scripture who can believe such gross stupidity. He's wearing yellow hose.

SIR TOBY Are they crossed at the knee and tied in a bow?

MARIA Hideously, like a church-school teacher. I have stalked him like a murderer. He has followed every lead in my anonymous letter. His smiling face breaks into more creases than the lines in a map showing the West Indies. You haven't seen the like. I want to throw rocks at him. I know the Countess will hit him. If she does, he will smile at her as though she did him a favor.

SIR TOBY Take us to him. *[FABIAN and SIR TOBY follow MARIA out of the room.]*

ACT III, SCENE 3

A street.

[Enter SEBASTIAN and ANTONIO]

SEBASTIAN I would not by my will have troubled you;
But, since you make your pleasure of your pains,
I will no further chide you.

ANTONIO I could not stay behind you. My desire,
More sharp than filed steel, did spur me forth;
And not all love to see you, though so much
As might have drawn one to a longer voyage,
But jealousy what might befall your travel,
Being skilless in these parts, which to a stranger,
Unguided and unfriended, often prove
Rough and unhospitable. My willing love,
The rather by these arguments of fear,
Set forth in your pursuit.

SEBASTIAN My kind Antonio,
I can no other answer make but thanks,
And thanks, and ever thanks. Often good turns
Are shuffled off with such uncurrent pay;
But, were my worth as is my conscience firm,
You should find better dealing. What's to do?
Shall we go see the reliques of this town?

ANTONIO To-morrow, sir. Best first go see your lodging.

SEBASTIAN I am not weary, and 'tis long to night.
I pray you, let us satisfy our eyes
With the memorials and the things of fame
That do renown this city.

ANTONIO Would you'ld pardon me;
I do not without danger walk these streets.
Once, in a sea-fight, 'gainst the count his galleys
I did some service; of such note indeed,
That were I ta'en here it would scarce be answer'd.

SEBASTIAN Belike you slew great number of his people.

ACT III, SCENE 3

A street in Illyria.

[SEBASTIAN and ANTONIO enter.]

SEBASTIAN I would not selfishly trouble you. But since you enjoy suffering, I won't scold you.

ANTONIO I could not let you go on alone. My sharpened will sent me after you. It wasn't just my wish to see you, which would make me travel even farther. I was suspicious of misadventures that might befall a friendly newcomer who is unaccustomed to this rough, inhospitable country. More than fear, friendship sent me in pursuit.

SEBASTIAN Dear Antonio, I have no reply but many thanks. Sometimes people brush off good deeds without gratitude. If my monetary worth were as secure as my conscience, you would be better rewarded. What shall we do? Shall we tour the old part of town?

ANTONIO We can tomorrow. First, let's find you a place to stay.

SEBASTIAN I'm not tired. It's a long time until night. Please, let's enjoy the city's monuments and landmarks.

ANTONIO Excuse me. It is dangerous for me in the streets. I once fought in a sea battle against Duke Orsino's ships. I made such a name for myself that, if I were arrested, I couldn't deny being his enemy.

SEBASTIAN Did you kill many of his men?

ANTONIO The offence is not of such a bloody nature;
Albeit the quality of the time and quarrel
Might well have given us bloody argument.
It might have since been answer'd in repaying
What we took from them, which, for traffic's sake,
Most of our city did. Only myself stood out;
For which, if I be lapsed in his place,
I shall pay dear.

SEBASTIAN Do not then walk to open.

ANTONIO It doth not fit me. Hold, sir, here's my purse.
In the south suburbs, at the Elephant,
Is best to lodge. I will bespeak our diet,
Whiles you beguile the time and feed your knowledge
With viewing of the town. There shall you have me.

SEBASTIAN Why I your purse?

ANTONIO Haply your eye shall light upon some toy
You have desire to purchase; and your store,
I think is not for idle markets, sir.

SEBASTIAN I'll be your purse-bearer and leave you
For an hour.

ANTONIO To the Elephant.

SEBASTIAN I do remember.

[Exeunt]

ANTONIO My actions were not murderous. However, the clash and its hostilities could have caused a bloody fight. I might have atoned by repaying what I stole from him. Most businessmen in the city paid him back. I was the only one who refused. If I fall into his hands, I will pay dearly.

SEBASTIAN Don't walk in the open.

ANTONIO It is not a good idea. Wait. Take my wallet. In the southern outskirts, you can room comfortably at the Elephant. While you spend your time touring the town, I will order our dinner. Meet me there.

SEBASTIAN Why should I take your wallet?

ANTONIO Perhaps you will find a bauble to buy. You don't have enough money to waste on trinkets.

SEBASTIAN I will sightsee for an hour with your wallet in hand.

ANTONIO Meet me at the Elephant.

SEBASTIAN I will remember. *[ANTONIO and SEBASTIAN depart.]*

ACT III, SCENE 4

Olivia's garden.

[Enter OLIVIA and MARIA]

OLIVIA I have sent after him; he says he'll come.
How shall I feast him? what bestow of him?
For youth is bought more oft than begg'd or borrow'd.
I speak too loud. Where is Malvolio? he is sad and civil,
And suits well for a servant with my fortunes.
Where is Malvolio?

MARIA He's coming, madam; but in very strange manner. He is, sure, possessed, madam.

OLIVIA Why, what's the matter? does he rave?

MARIA No, madam, he does nothing but smile. Your ladyship were best to have some guard about you, if he come; for, sure, the man is tainted in 's wits.

OLIVIA Go call him hither. *[Exit MARIA]* I am as mad as he,
If sad and merry madness equal be.
[Re-enter MARIA, with MALVOLIO]
How now, Malvolio!

MALVOLIO Sweet lady, ho, ho.

OLIVIA Smilest thou?
I sent for thee upon a sad occasion.

MALVOLIO Sad, lady! I could be sad. This does make some obstruction in the blood, this cross-gartering; but what of that? if it please the eye of one, it is with me as the very true sonnet is, "Please one, and please all."

OLIVIA Why, how dost thou, man? what is the matter with thee?

MALVOLIO Not black in my mind, though yellow in my legs. It did come to his hands, and commands shall be executed. I think we do know the sweet Roman hand.

OLIVIA God comfort thee! Why dost thou smile so and kiss thy hand so oft?

ACT III, SCENE 4

The Countess Olivia's garden.

[OLIVIA and MARIA enter.]

OLIVIA I sent for Cesario. He said he would come. What shall I serve for dinner? What gifts shall I give him? It is often easier to buy young men than to beg or borrow them. I speak too loud. Where is Malvolio? He is sober and mannerly. He is a suitable servant for a woman in my position. Where is Malvolio?

MARIA He is coming, ma'am, but he doesn't look like his usual self. He must be bewitched.

OLIVIA What's the matter with him? Is he insane?

MARIA No, ma'am, he is only smiling. Keep up your guard when he comes. Surely, his sanity is touched.

OLIVIA Summon him here. *[MARIA departs.]* I am as crazy as he is if sadness and joy add up to insanity.
[MARIA returns with MALVOLIO.]
How are you, Malvolio!

MALVOLIO Sweet lady, ho, ho.

OLIVIA Why are you smiling? I sent for you on a serious matter.

MALVOLIO Serious? I can be serious. Tying my garters around my knee cuts off my blood circulation, but I don't mind. If you like them, I am happy with them. As the poem says, "What pleases one person pleases everybody."

OLIVIA Why are you behaving like this? What is wrong with you?

MALVOLIO There are no dark thoughts in my mind, only yellow hose on my legs. I received the letter, and I am doing as it commanded. I recognized the Italian handwriting.

OLIVIA God take care of you! Why do you smile and throw kisses?

MARIA How do you, Malvolio?

MALVOLIO At your request? Yes, nightingales answer daws.

MARIA Why appear you with this ridiculous boldness before my lady?

MALVOLIO 'Be not afraid of greatness.' 'Twas well writ.

OLIVIA What meanest thou by that, Malvolio?

MALVOLIO 'Some are born great.'

OLIVIA Ha!

MALVOLIO 'Some achieve greatness.'

OLIVIA What sayest thou?

MALVOLIO 'And some have greatness thrust upon them.'

OLIVIA Heaven restore thee!

MALVOLIO 'Remember who commended thy yellow stockings.'

OLIVIA Thy yellow stockings!

MALVOLIO 'And wished to see thee cross-gartered.'

OLIVIA Cross-gartered!

MALVOLIO 'Go to, thou art made, if thou desirest to be so.'

OLIVIA Am I made?

MALVOLIO 'If not, let me see thee a servant still.'

OLIVIA Why, this is very midsummer madness.
[Enter SERVANT]

SERVANT Madam, the young gentleman of the Count Orsino's is returned. I could hardly entreat him back. He attends your ladyship's pleasure.

OLIVIA I'll come to him. *[Exit SERVANT]* Good Maria, let this fellow be looked to. Where's my cousin Toby? Let some of my people have a special care of him. I would not have him miscarry for the half of my dowry.
[Exeunt OLIVIA and MARIA]

MARIA How are you, Malvolio?

MALVOLIO Do you question me? Well, nightingales may reply to blackbirds like you.

MARIA Why are you so insulting in front of the Countess?

MALVOLIO The letter said, "Don't fear my rank." That was good advice.

OLIVIA What are you talking about, Malvolio?

MALVOLIO It said, "Some people are great at birth."

OLIVIA What?

MALVOLIO It said, "Some make themselves great."

OLIVIA What do you mean?

MALVOLIO It said, "Some find advancement by accident."

OLIVIA God heal you!

MALVOLIO It said, "Think of me as the person who liked you in yellow hose."

OLIVIA Your yellow hose!

MALVOLIO It said, "And who wanted to see you tie your garters around your knee in a bow."

OLIVIA Your garters tied around your knee?

MALVOLIO It said, "If you like this proposition, then accept it."

OLIVIA Am I tricked?

MALVOLIO It said, "If not, stay a steward."

OLIVIA This is midsummer nuttiness. *[A SERVANT enters.]*

SERVANT Madam, Cesario has returned. I could hardly beg him to come back. He awaits your orders.

OLIVIA I'll go to him. *[The SERVANT departs.]* Maria, find help for Malvolio. Where is Toby? Let the staff take care of Malvolio. I wouldn't want him harmed for half my dowry. *[OLIVIA and MARIA depart.]*

MALVOLIO Oho! do you come near me now? no worse man than Sir Toby to look to me! This concurs directly with the letter: she sends him on purpose, that I may appear stubborn to him; for she incites me to that in the letter. 'Cast thy humble slough,' says she; 'be opposite with a kinsman, surly with servants; let thy tongue tang with arguments of state; put thyself into the trick of singularity'; and consequently sets down the manner how: as, a sad face, a reverend carriage, a slow tongue, in the habit of some sir of note, and so forth. I have limed her; but it is Jove's doing, and Jove make me thankful! And when she went away now, 'Let this fellow be looked to.' 'Fellow!' not Malvolio, nor after my degree, but 'fellow.' Why, everything adheres together, that no dram of a scruple, no scruple of a scruple, no obstacle, no incredulous or unsafe circumstance—What can be said? Nothing that can be can come between me and the full prospect of my hopes. Well, Jove, not I, is the doer of this, and he is to be thanked.

[Re-enter MARIA, with SIR TOBY and FABIAN]

SIR TOBY Which way is he, in the name of sanctity? If all the devils of hell be drawn in little, and Legion himself possessed him, yet I'll speak to him.

FABIAN Here he is, here he is. How is't with you, sir? how is't with you, man?

MALVOLIO Go off; I discard you. Let me enjoy my private. Go off.

MARIA Lo, how hollow the fiend speaks within him! Did not I tell you? Sir Toby, my lady prays you to have a care of him.

MALVOLIO Aha! does she so?

SIR TOBY Go to, go to; peace, peace; we must deal gently with him. Let me alone. How do you, Malvolio? how is't with you? What, man! defy the devil. Consider, he's an enemy to mankind.

MALVOLIO Do you know what you say?

MALVOLIO Oho! Do you see how I've advanced? She is sending her uncle Toby to care for me! This is what the letter promised. She sends him to me so I can be firm with him. That's what the letter indicated. The letter said, "Give up your lowly state." "Quarrel with relatives, grumble at servants. Venture into political discussions. Think like an individual." She even tells me how to do all this. I should wear a somber expression, a dignified posture, limit my words like a noteworthy man, and so forth. I have caught her. Jupiter won her for me. I am grateful to Jupiter. When she just went out, she ordered, "Find help for this fellow." She called me "fellow," not Malvolio the steward, but "fellow." Everything is coming together. There is not an ounce of doubt, no drop of an ounce, no obstacle, no suspicion or faulty clue. What can I say? Nothing can separate me and my desire. Jupiter did this for me. I must thank him. *[MARIA returns with SIR TOBY and FABIAN.]*

SIR TOBY Where is Malvolio, in the name of all that is holy? If all of hell's demons were pressed into a dot and Satan himself possessed Malvolio, I wouldn't miss this chance to speak to him.

FABIAN Here he is, here he is. How are you, sir? Are you well?

MALVOLIO Go away. Leave me. I want my privacy. Go.

MARIA Listen to the hollow demon inside him! Didn't I warn you? Sir Toby, the Countess wants you to take care of Malvolio.

MALVOLIO Really? She does?

SIR TOBY Stop. Hush. We must be gentle with him. Leave me alone with him. Hello, Malvolio. Are you well? Fight this demon inside of you. Remember that he threatens all humanity.

MALVOLIO What are you saying?

MARIA La you, an you speak ill of the devil, how he takes it at heart! Pray God, he be not bewitched! My lady would not lose him for more than I'll say.

MALVOLIO How now, mistress!

MARIA O Lord!

SIR TOBY Prithee, hold thy peace; this is not the way. Do you not see you move him? let me alone with him.

FABIAN No way but gentleness; gently, gently. The fiend is rough, and will not be roughly used.

SIR TOBY Why, how now, my bawcock! how dost thou, chuck?

MALVOLIO Sir!

SIR TOBY Ay, Biddy, come with me. What, man! 'tis not for gravity to play at cherry-pit with Satan. Hang him, foul collier!

MARIA Get him to say his prayers, good Sir Toby, get him to pray.

MALVOLIO My prayers, minx!

MARIA No, I warrant you, he will not hear of godliness.

MALVOLIO Go, hang yourselves all! you are idle shallow things; I am not of your element. You shall know more hereafter.
[Exit]

SIR TOBY Is't possible?

FABIAN If this were played upon a stage now, I could condemn it as an improbable fiction.

SIR TOBY His very genius hath taken the infection of the device, man.

MARIA Nay, pursue him now, lest the device take air and taint.

FABIAN Why, we shall make him mad indeed.

MARIA The house will be the quieter.

MARIA Notice that if you provoke Satan, Malvolio is insulted. Please, God, don't let Malvolio be possessed! The Countess would not give up Malvolio for anything.

MALVOLIO What are you saying, Maria!

MARIA Oh, Lord!

SIR TOBY Please, don't talk. This is not working. Don't you realize that you upset him? Leave me alone with him.

FABIAN Be gentle with him. Easy, easy. Satan is harsh and refuses to be challenged.

SIR TOBY How are you, old pal! How are you, buddy?

MALVOLIO Sir!

SIR TOBY Come with me, little one. Please don't play games with Satan. Kill the evil one!

MARIA Ask him to say his prayers, Sir Toby. Ask him to pray.

MALVOLIO Say my prayers, you hussy!

MARIA I promise you that Malvolio will have no part in piety.

MALVOLIO Be hanged, all of you. You are silly nothings. I am above your status. You will find out later. *[MALVOLIO departs.]*

SIR TOBY I can't believe it.

FABIAN If this were a play, I would think it stranger than fiction.

SIR TOBY The anonymous letter has twisted him.

MARIA Follow him. Don't let anybody see him and spoil our fun.

FABIAN We will surely drive him crazy.

MARIA The house will be quieter without him.

SIR TOBY Come, we'll have him in a dark room and bound. My niece is already in the belief that he's mad. We may carry it thus, for our pleasure and his penance, till our very pastime, tired out of breath, prompt us to have mercy on him, at which time we will bring the device to the bar and crown thee for a finder of madmen. But see, but see!
[Enter SIR ANDREW]

FABIAN More matter for a May morning.

SIR ANDREW Here's the challenge, read it. I warrant there's vinegar and pepper in't.

FABIAN Is't so saucy?

SIR ANDREW Ay, is't, I warrant him. Do but read.

SIR TOBY Give me. *[Reads]* 'Youth, whatsoever thou art, thou art but a scurvy fellow.'

FABIAN Good, and valiant.

SIR TOBY *[Reads]* 'Wonder not, nor admire not in thy mind, why I do call thee so, for I will show thee no reason for't.'

FABIAN A good note; that keeps you from the blow of the law.

SIR TOBY *[Reads]* 'Thou comest to the Lady Olivia, and in my sight she uses thee kindly; but thou liest in thy throat. That is not the matter I challenge thee for.'

FABIAN Very brief, and to exceeding good sense—less.

SIR TOBY *[Reads]* 'I will waylay thee going home, where if it be thy chance to kill me'—

FABIAN Good.

SIR TOBY *[Reads]* 'Thou killest me like a rogue and a villain.'

FABIAN Still you keep o' the windy side of the law; good.

SIR TOBY *[Reads]* 'Fare thee well; and God have mercy upon one of our souls! He may have mercy upon mine; but my hope is better, and so look to thyself. Thy friend, as thou usest him, and thy sworn enemy, Andrew Aguecheek.' If this letter move him not, his legs cannot. I'll give it him.

SIR TOBY Let's tie him up and shut him in a dark room. The Countess already believes that he's insane. We can keep up the joke for our enjoyment and his punishment until we take pity on him. We will take the case to court and reward Maria for apprehending a maniac. Look here! *[SIR ANDREW enters.]*

FABIAN More opportunity for Mayday fun.

SIR ANDREW Here is my challenge to Cesario. Read it. I guarantee that it's spicy.

FABIAN Is it rude?

SIR ANDREW Yes, it is to him. Here, read it.

SIR TOBY Let me read it. *[SIR TOBY reads aloud SIR ANDREW's challenge to CESARIO.]* "Young man, whoever you are, you are a low-life."

FABIAN Good beginning and brave.

SIR TOBY *[SIR TOBY continues reading SIR ANDREW's challenge.]* "Don't be surprised that I challenge you. I will give you no reason to be surprised."

FABIAN A good point. That will spare you an arrest for slander.

SIR TOBY *[SIR TOBY continues reading.]* "When you visit the Countess Olivia, she is polite to you, but you lie to her. That is not why I demand a duel."

FABIAN Nice and short and to the point—*[FABIAN adds in a whisper]*—less.

SIR TOBY *[SIR TOBY continues reading.]* "I will ambush you on the road and give you a shot at me."

FABIAN That sounds good.

SIR TOBY *[SIR TOBY continues reading.]* "You would murder me like a criminal and a felon."

FABIAN You still protect yourself from arrest. That's good.

SIR TOBY *[SIR TOBY continues reading.]* "Good-bye. And God pity one of us! He may pity me more, but I have high hopes and intend to protect myself. Your friend, if you think him a friend, and your enemy, Andrew Aguecheek." If this letter doesn't stir him up, his legs won't move. I'll send it to Cesario.

MARIA You may have very fit occasion for't; he is now in some commerce with my lady, and will by and by depart.

SIR TOBY Go, Sir Andrew; scout me for him at the corner of the orchard like a bum-baily. So soon as ever thou seest him, draw; and, as thou drawest, swear horrible; for it comes to pass oft that a terrible oath, with a swaggering accent sharply twanged off, gives manhood more approbation than ever proof itself would have earned him. Away!

SIR ANDREW Nay, let me alone for swearing.
[Exit]

SIR TOBY Now will not I deliver his letter: for the behaviour of the young gentleman gives him out to be of good capacity and breeding; his employment between his lord and my niece confirms no less. Therefore this letter, being so excellently ignorant, will breed no terror in the youth. He will find it comes from a clodpole. But, sir, I will deliver his challenge by word of mouth; set upon Aguecheek a notable report of valour; and drive the gentleman, as I know his youth will aptly receive it, into a most hideous opinion of his rage, skill, fury and impetuosity. This will so fright them both that they will kill one another by the look, like cockatrices.
[Re-enter OLIVIA, with VIOLA]

FABIAN Here he comes with your niece; give them way till he take leave, and presently after him.

SIR TOBY I will meditate the while upon some horrid message for a challenge.
[Exeunt SIR TOBY, FABIAN, and MARIA]

OLIVIA
I have said too much unto a heart of stone
And laid mine honour too unchary out.
There's something in me that reproves my fault;
But such a headstrong potent fault it is,
That it but mocks reproof.

VIOLA
With the same 'haviour that your passion bears
Goes on my master's grief.

MARIA You may have an opportunity today. He has business with the Countess and will soon be leaving.

SIR TOBY Check on it, Sir Andrew. Like a deputy sheriff, scout him out at the corner of the orchard. As soon as he appears, draw your sword. While you hold your weapon, curse him. Swearing in a bold voice often makes a man seem meaner than he is. Go!

SIR ANDREW Don't worry about my cursing. *[SIR ANDREW goes out.]*

SIR TOBY Now I will deliver the challenge to Cesario. He acts like a well bred, intelligent gentleman. His service as ambassador from Duke Orsino to the Countess proves Cesario worthy. This ignorant letter will not alarm him. He will realize that it is the writing of a knothead. I will deliver Cesario's reply verbally. I will report to Sir Andrew on Cesario's courage. I will terrify Cesario with lies about Sir Andrew's rage, skill, fury, and hotheadedness. Both duelers will be so scared that they will collapse when they meet. *[The COUNTESS OLIVIA returns with VIOLA disguised as CESARIO.]*

FABIAN Here comes Cesario with the Countess. Let them finish their business, then follow Cesario.

SIR TOBY I will think up some terrifying challenge from Sir Andrew. *[SIR TOBY, FABIAN, and MARIA depart.]*

OLIVIA I waste words on a stony heart and am too free with myself. I shame myself for my boldness. But my will is so strong that it refuses to be controlled.

VIOLA Your reply is as passionate as my master's suffering.

OLIVIA Here, wear this jewel for me, 'tis my picture.
Refuse it not; it hath no tongue to vex you;
And I beseech you come again to-morrow.
What shall you ask of me that I'll deny,
That honour saved may upon asking give?

VIOLA Nothing but this, your true love for my master.

OLIVIA How with mine honour may I give him that
Which I have given to you?

VIOLA I will acquit you.

OLIVIA Well, come again to-morrow. Fare thee well.
[Exit]
[Re-enter SIR TOBY and FABIAN]

SIR TOBY Gentleman, God save thee.

VIOLA And you, sir.

SIR TOBY That defence thou hast, betake thee to't. Of what nature the wrongs are thou hast done him, I know not; but thy intercepter, full of despite, bloody as the hunter, attends thee at the orchard-end. Dismount thy tuck, be yare in the preparation, for thy assailant is quick, skilful, and deadly.

VIOLA You mistake, sir; I am sure no man hath any quarrel to me. My remembrance is very free and clear from any image of offence done to any man.

SIR TOBY You'll find it otherwise, I assure you. Therefore, if you hold your life at any price, betake you to your guard; for your opposite hath in him what youth, strength, skill, and wrath can furnish man withal.

VIOLA I pray you, sir, what is he?

SIR TOBY He is knight, dubbed with unhatched rapier and on carpet consideration; but he is a devil in private brawl. Souls and bodies hath he divorced three; and his incensement at this moment is so implacable, that satisfaction can be none but by pangs of death and sepulchre. Hob, nob, is his word; give't or take't.

VIOLA I will return again into the house and desire some conduct of the lady. I am no fighter. I have heard of some kind of men that put quarrels purposely on others, to taste their valour. Belike this is a man of that quirk.

OLIVIA	Here is a brooch with my picture inside. Please take it. It has no words to annoy you. Please come back tomorrow. What could you ask of me that I would not honorably give you?
VIOLA	Only one thing—that you love Duke Orsino.
OLIVIA	How can I love him when I love you?
VIOLA	I release you from loving me.
OLIVIA	Come back tomorrow. Good-bye. *[The COUNTESS OLIVIA returns to the house.]* *[SIR TOBY and FABIAN approach CESARIO.]*
SIR TOBY	Greetings, sir.
VIOLA	And to you, sir.
SIR TOBY	You must defend yourself. I don't know how you have insulted Sir Andrew. He waits in ambush at the end of the orchard, spiteful and bloodthirsty. Hurry, draw your sword. Your enemy is quick, skillful, and deadly.
VIOLA	You must be mistaken. I have no enemy. I haven't insulted any man.
SIR TOBY	You have an enemy, I assure you. If you want to live, be careful. Your opponent is young, strong, skillful, and furious.
VIOLA	Who is this man?
SIR TOBY	He is a warrior knighted on a carpet with an unused sword. He is a vicious brawler. He has killed three victims. He is so enraged that he won't stop until he has killed and buried you. Hit or miss is his attitude. Kill or be killed.
VIOLA	I will return to the Countess to request safe passage home. I am not a swordsman. I have heard of men who make up insults just to satisfy their bloodlust. This man must like to pick fights.

SIR TOBY Sir, no; his indignation derives itself out of a very competent injury. Therefore, get you on and give him his desire. Back you shall not to the house, unless you undertake that with me which with as much safety you might answer him. Therefore, on, or strip your sword stark naked; for meddle you must, that's certain, or forswear to wear iron about you.

VIOLA This is as uncivil as strange. I beseech you, do me this courteous office, as to know of the knight what my offence to him is. It is something of my negligence, nothing of my purpose.

SIR TOBY I will do so. Signior Fabian, stay you by this gentleman till my return.
[Exit]

VIOLA Pray you, sir, do you know of this matter?

FABIAN I know the knight is incensed against you, even to a mortal arbitrement; but nothing of the circumstance more.

VIOLA I beseech you, what manner of man is he?

FABIAN Nothing of that wonderful promise, to read him by his form, as you are like to find him in the proof of his valour. He is, indeed, sir, the most skilful, bloody, and fatal opposite that you could possibly have found in any part of Illyria. Will you walk towards him? I will make your peace with him if I can.

VIOLA I shall be much bound to you for't. I am one that had rather go with sir priest than sir knight. I care not who knows so much of my mettle.
[Exeunt]
[Re-enter SIR TOBY, with SIR ANDREW]

SIR TOBY Why, man, he's a very devil; I have not seen such a firago. I had a pass with him, rapier, scabbard, and all, and he gives me the stuck in with such a mortal motion, that it is inevitable; and on the answer, he pays you as surely as your feet hit the ground they step on. They say he has been fencer to the Sophy.

SIR ANDREW I'll not meddle with him.

SIR TOBY Ay, but he will not now be pacified. Fabian can scarce hold him yonder.

SIR TOBY No, he has good reason for challenging you. Go fight him and satisfy his anger. You won't return alive unless you prepare to fight him. Out with your sword! If you don't accept the challenge, you can never again carry a weapon.

VIOLA This is as crude as it is weird. Tell me how I insulted this knight. It must be some unintentional slight.

SIR TOBY I will find out. Fabian, stay with Cesario until I return. *[SIR TOBY goes out.]*

VIOLA What do you know about this challenge, Fabian?

FABIAN I know that the knight is mad enough to kill you. I don't know his reason for rage.

VIOLA Tell me about him.

FABIAN You can see in his expression that he is brave. He's the best dueler and the most dangerous scrapper in Illyria. Shall we meet him at the orchard? I will settle this argument if I can.

VIOLA I would be grateful to you if you could. I would rather face a priest than a warrior. I don't care what people think of my courage. *[FABIAN and CESARIO depart for the orchard.]*
[SIR TOBY returns to the COUNTESS's house with SIR ANDREW.]

SIR TOBY Sir, Cesario is a demon. I haven't seen such a fighter. I once faced him with a rapier. He strikes with such a thrust that nothing can stop him. On the second pass, he retaliates before his opponent can advance. It is rumored that he taught fencing to the ruler of Persia.

SIR ANDREW I won't challenge Cesario.

SIR TOBY He won't give up the challenge. Fabian can barely hold him back.

SIR ANDREW Plague on't, an' I thought he had been valiant and so cunning in fence, I'ld not have challenged him. Let him let the matter slip, and I'll give him my horse, gray Capilet.

SIR TOBY I'll make the motion. Stand here, make a good show on't; this shall end without the perdition of souls. *[aside]* Marry, I'll ride your horse as well as I ride you.
[Re-enter FABIAN and VIOLA]
[To FABIAN] I have his horse to take up the quarrel; I have persuaded him the youth's a devil.

FABIAN He is as horribly conceited of him; and pants and looks pale, as if a bear were at his heels.

SIR TOBY *[To VIOLA]* There's no remedy, sir; he will fight with you for oath's sake. Marry, he hath better bethought him of his quarrel, and he finds that now scarce to be worth talking of; therefore draw, for the supportance of his vow. He protests he will not hurt you.

VIOLA *[aside]* Pray God defend me! A little thing would make me tell them how much I lack of a man.

FABIAN Give ground, if you see him furious.

SIR TOBY Come, Sir Andrew, there's no remedy; the gentleman will, for his honour's sake, have one bout with you; he cannot by the duello avoid it. But he has promised me, as he is a gentleman and a soldier, he will not hurt you. Come on; to't.

SIR ANDREW Pray God, he keep his oath!

VIOLA I do assure you, 'tis against my will.
[They draw]
[Enter ANTONIO]

ANTONIO Put up your sword. If this young gentleman
Have done offence, I take the fault on me.
If you offend him, I for him defy you.

SIR TOBY You, sir! why, what are you?

ANTONIO One, sir, that for his love dares yet do more
Than you have heard him brag to you he will.

SIR TOBY Nay, if you be an undertaker, I am for you.
[They draw]
[Enter OFFICERS]

SIR ANDREW Drat. If I had known he was so hardy and clever a dueler, I wouldn't have challenged him. If Cesario will drop the matter, I will give him my horse, Little Gray Prancer.

SIR TOBY I will make the offer. Stay here and put on a grim face. This duel will end without loss of life. *[In private.]* I could ride Little Prancer as easily as I manipulate you. *[FABIAN and VIOLA disguised as CESARIO return.]* *[SIR TOBY to FABIAN.]* Sir Andrew offers his horse to settle the matter. I have convinced him that Cesario is a hellish fighter.

FABIAN Cesario is equally terrified of Sir Andrew. He pants and turns white as if a bear chased him.

SIR TOBY *[To VIOLA disguised as CESARIO.]* I can't settle this with words. Sir Andrew will fight you as he promised. He should reconsider the challenge. He admits that the insult was minor. Draw your weapon for the sake of his honor. He promises not to harm you.

VIOLA *[In private.]* God protect me! A small wound would reveal that I am really a woman.

FABIAN Back off if he seems enraged.

SIR TOBY Come, Sir Andrew. Cesario won't give in. He will defend his honor in one clash. According to dueling rules, he can't avoid a fight. He promised on his word as a gentleman and a soldier that he won't hurt you. Come on. Begin the duel.

SIR ANDREW Please, God, let Cesario keep his word not to hurt me!

VIOLA I assure you that you force me to fight. *[CESARIO and SIR ANDREW draw swords.]* *[ANTONIO appears.]*

ANTONIO Stop the duel. If this young man has insulted you, fight me instead. If you insulted him, I will attack you in his place.

SIR TOBY You? Who are you?

ANTONIO Out of friendship, I will do more harm to you than he promised to do.

SIR TOBY Even if you are a mortician, I will fight you. *[ANTONIO and SIR TOBY draw swords.]* *[OFFICERS arrive.]*

FABIAN O good Sir Toby, hold! here come the officers.

SIR TOBY *[To ANTONIO]* I'll be with you anon.

VIOLA Pray, sir, put your sword up, if you please.

SIR ANDREW Marry, will I, sir; and for that I promised you, I'll be as good as my word. He will bear you easily and reins well.

FIRST OFFICER This is the man; do thy office.

SECOND OFFICER Antonio, I arrest thee at the suit of Count Orsino.

ANTONIO You do mistake me, sir.

FIRST OFFICER No, sir, no jot; I know your favour well,
Though now you have no sea-cap on your head.
Take him away; he knows I know him well.

ANTONIO I must obey. *[To VIOLA]* This comes with seeking you:
But there's no remedy; I shall answer it.
What will you do, now my necessity
Makes me to ask you for my purse? It grieves me
Much more for what I cannot do for you
Than what befalls myself. You stand amazed;
But be of comfort.

SECOND OFFICER Come, sir, away.

ANTONIO I must entreat of you some of that money.

VIOLA What money, sir?
For the fair kindness you have show'd me here,
And, part, being prompted by your present trouble,
Out of my lean and low ability
I'll lend you something. My having is not much;
I'll make division of my present with you.
Hold, there's half my coffer.

ANTONIO Will you deny me now?
Is't possible that my deserts to you
Can lack persuasion? Do not tempt my misery,
Lest that it make me so unsound a man
As to upbraid you with those kindnesses
That I have done for you.

FABIAN Sir Toby, here come the police.

SIR TOBY *[SIR TOBY to ANTONIO.]* I'll be right back.

VIOLA Please, Sir Toby, put up your weapon.

SIR ANDREW Gladly. I give you my horse, just as I promised. He will ride smoothly and obey your control.

FIRST OFFICER This is the man. Arrest him.

SECOND OFFICER Antonio, I arrest you on a warrant from Duke Orsino.

ANTONIO You are making a mistake.

FIRST OFFICER No, there's no mistake. I recognize your face even without your captain's hat. Take him to jail. He knows I recognize him.

ANTONIO I must obey the police. *[ANTONIO to VIOLA disguised as CESARIO.]* It is my fault for following you. It is too late now. I must go to jail. How will you manage? I must have my wallet back. I am sorry that I can't protect you any more than I can protect myself. You look surprised. Don't worry.

SECOND OFFICER Come with me.

ANTONIO I must have some of my money back.

VIOLA What money? You have been kind to me. Because of your dilemma, I will lend you what little I have. I don't have much. I will give you a share. Here's half of it.

ANTONIO Are you refusing to help me? Are all my courtesies to you unimportant? Don't annoy me now. You anger me into shaming you for discounting my kindness.

VIOLA I know of none;
Nor know I you by voice or any feature.
I hate ingratitude more in a man
Than lying vainness, babbling drunkenness,
Or any taint of vice whose strong corruption
Inhabits our frail blood.

ANTONIO O heavens themselves!

SECOND OFFICER Come, sir, I pray you, go.

ANTONIO Let me speak a little. This youth that you see here
I snatch'd one half out of the jaws of death,
Relieved him with such sanctity of love,
And to his image, which methought did promise
Most venerable worth, did I devotion.

FIRST OFFICER What's that to us? The time goes by; away!

ANTONIO But oh, how vile an idol proves this god!
Thou hast, Sebastian, done good feature shame.
In nature there's no blemish but the mind;
None can be called deform'd but the unkind;
Virtue is beauty, but the beauteous-evil
Are empty trunks o'erflourish'd by the devil.

FIRST OFFICER The man grows mad; away with him!
Come, come, sir.

ANTONIO Lead me on.
[Exit with OFFICERS]

VIOLA Methinks his words do from such passion fly,
That he believes himself. So do not I.
Prove true, imagination, O prove true,
That I, dear brother, be now ta'en for you!

SIR TOBY Come hither, knight; come hither, Fabian; we'll whisper o'er a couplet or two of most sage saws.

VIOLA He named Sebastian. I my brother know
Yet living in my glass; even such and so
In favour was my brother, and he went
Still in this fashion, colour, ornament,
For him I imitate. Oh, if it prove,
Tempests are kind and salt waves fresh in love.

[Exit]

VIOLA I know of no kindness. I don't recognize your face or voice. I hate ungratefulness more than vanity, drunkenness, or any other vice that corrupts the character.

ANTONIO Oh God!

SECOND OFFICER Come with me, sir.

ANTONIO Let me say more. I rescued this young man from death. I offered friendship and loyalty to a person I thought worthy.

FIRST OFFICER Why should we care? It's late. Let's go!

ANTONIO But this man has turned against me! You have, Sebastian, shamed yourself. Your fault is in your mind. Your fault is unkindness. Goodness is beautiful. The evil handsome man is an empty box decorated on the outside by Satan.

FIRST OFFICER Antonio is raving. Take him away! Come, sir.

ANTONIO I'm going. *[ANTONIO departs with the police.]*

VIOLA His statements erupt from anger. He believes what he says. I don't. Oh, Sebastian, is it possible that I pass for you?

SIR TOBY Come here, Sir Andrew. Come here, Fabian. Let's share some wise sayings.

VIOLA Antonio called me Sebastian. My brother must be alive and recognizable in my face. He looked like me. I imitated the way he dressed. If I am right, the sea spared him. *[VIOLA goes out.]*

SIR TOBY A very dishonest paltry boy, and more a coward than a hare. His dishonesty appears in leaving his friend here in necessity and denying him; and for his cowardship, ask Fabian.

FABIAN A coward, a most devout coward, religious in it.

SIR ANDREW 'Slid, I'll after him again and beat him.

SIR TOBY Do; cuff him soundly, but never draw thy sword.

SIR ANDREW An I do not, —
[Exit]

FABIAN Come, let's see the event.

SIR TOBY I dare lay any money 'twill be nothing yet.
[Exeunt]

SIR TOBY Cesario is insincere and as cowardly as a rabbit. He proves himself rude by abandoning his friend and refusing him money. Fabian witnessed his gutlessness.

FABIAN A coward, a yellow coward devoted to running away.

SIR ANDREW God's eyelid, I'll chase him down and beat him.

SIR TOBY Yes. Whip him soundly. But don't use your sword.

SIR ANDREW If I fail— *[SIR ANDREW departs.]*

FABIAN Come on. Let's watch.

SIR TOBY I'll bet money this fight will come to nothing. *[FABIAN and SIR TOBY depart.]*

ACT IV, SCENE 1

The street before Olivia's house.

[Enter SEBASTIAN and CLOWN]

CLOWN Will you make me believe that I am not sent for you?

SEBASTIAN Go to, go to, thou art a foolish fellow.
Let me be clear of thee.

CLOWN Well held out, i' faith! No, I do not know you; nor I am not sent to you by my lady, to bid you come speak with her; nor your name is not Master Cesario; nor this is not my nose neither. Nothing that is so is so.

SEBASTIAN I prithee, vent thy folly somewhere else;
Thou know'st not me.

CLOWN Vent my folly! he has heard that word of some great man, and now applies it to a fool. Vent my folly! I am afraid this great lubber, the world, will prove a cockney. I prithee now, ungrid thy strangeness and tell me what I shall vent to my lady. Shall I vent to her that thou art coming?

SEBASTIAN I prithee, foolish Greek, depart from me.
There's money for thee; if you tarry longer,
I shall give worse payment.

CLOWN By my troth, thou hast an open hand. These wise men that give fools money get themselves a good report—after fourteen years' purchase.
[Enter SIR ANDREW, SIR TOBY and FABIAN]

SIR ANDREW Now, sir, have I met you again? there's for you.
[Striking SEBASTIAN]

SEBASTIAN Why, there's for thee, and there, and there.
Are all the people mad?
[Beating SIR ANDREW]

SIR TOBY Hold, sir, or I'll throw your dagger o'er the house.

CLOWN This will I tell my lady straight; I would not be in some of your coats for two pence.
[Exit]

SIR TOBY Come on, sir; hold.

ACT IV, SCENE 1

The street in front of the residence of the Countess Olivia in Illyria east of Italy.

[SEBASTIAN and FESTE the jester enter.]

CLOWN Are you pretending that you aren't the man I seek?

SEBASTIAN Stop, you are an idiot. Leave me alone.

CLOWN You are really stubborn. No, I don't know you. The Countess Olivia didn't send for you to speak with her. Your name isn't Cesario. And this isn't my nose. Nothing true is true.

SEBASTIAN Please, be a joker somewhere else. You don't know me.

CLOWN Be a joker! He has heard that term from a learned man and uses it against an entertainer. Be a joker! I fear that the world will prove this lout a moron. Give up your pretense. What shall I reply to the Countess Olivia? Shall I tell her you are coming to her house?

SEBASTIAN Please, stupid joker, go away. Here's a coin. If you won't leave, I will give you something you won't like.

CLOWN You are generous. Wise men who tip jesters earn a good reputation, maybe after fourteen years. *[SIR ANDREW, SIR TOBY and FABIAN enter.]*

SIR ANDREW Well, sir, do we meet again? Here's something for you. *[SIR ANDREW slaps SEBASTIAN.]*

SEBASTIAN Here's a few slaps for you. Are all Illyrians crazy? *[SEBASTIAN pummels SIR ANDREW.]*

SIR TOBY Stop or I will toss your dagger over the roof.

CLOWN I will report this to the Countess Olivia. I wouldn't be in your shoes for two cents. *[FESTE goes out.]*

SIR TOBY Stop, sir.

SIR ANDREW Nay, let him alone. I'll go another way to work with him. I'll have an action of battery against him, if there be any law in Illyria; though I struck him first, yet it's no matter for that.

SEBASTIAN Let go thy hand.

SIR TOBY Come, sir, I will not let you go. Come, my young soldier, put up your iron. You are well fleshed; come on.

SEBASTIAN I will be free from thee. What wouldst thou now?
If thou darest tempt me further, draw thy sword.

SIR TOBY What, what? Nay, then I must have an ounce
or two of this malapert blood from you.
[Enter OLIVIA]

OLIVIA Hold, Toby; on thy life I charge thee, hold!

SIR TOBY Madam!

OLIVIA Will it be ever thus? Ungracious wretch,
Fit for the mountains and the barbarous caves,
Where manners ne'er were preach'd! out of my sight!
Be not offended, dear Cesario.
Rudesby, be gone!
[Exeunt SIR TOBY, SIR ANDREW and FABIAN]
I prithee, gentle friend,
Let thy fair wisdom, not thy passion, sway
In this uncivil and unjust extent
Against thy peace. Go with me to my house,
And hear thou there how many fruitless pranks
This ruffian hath botch'd up, that thou thereby
Mayst smile at this. Thou shalt not choose but go.
Do not deny. Beshrew his soul for me,
He started one poor heart of mine in thee.

SEBASTIAN What relish is in this? how runs the stream?
Or I am mad, or else this is a dream.
Let fancy still my sense in Lethe steep;
If it be thus to dream, still let me sleep!

OLIVIA Nay, come, I prithee; would thou'dst be ruled by me!

SEBASTIAN Madam, I will.

OLIVIA Oh, say so, and so be!
[Exeunt]

SIR ANDREW Leave him alone. I'll help you fight him off. I'll have him arrested for street fighting, if Illyria has such a law. It doesn't matter that I started the fight.

SEBASTIAN Take your hand off me.

SIR TOBY I won't let go of you. Young warrior, drop your weapon. You've had enough combat. Stop.

SEBASTIAN Let me go. What do you want from me? If you taunt me any more, draw your weapon.

SIR TOBY What did you say? If you keep on wrangling, I will spill a few ounces of your blood. *[The COUNTESS OLIVIA enters.]*

OLIVIA Stop, Toby. Stop, if you value your life!

SIR TOBY Madam!

OLIVIA Are you always going to be a problem? Ungrateful wretch, you should live in the hills and caves where there are no manners. Out of my sight! Don't be insulted, Cesario. Boor, go away! *[SIR TOBY, SIR ANDREW, and FABIAN depart.]*
Please, good friend, don't let anger at this uproar upset you. Come into my house. I will tell you of all the pranks that Sir Toby has pulled. You may laugh at his silliness. You must come. Don't refuse. Forgive him for my sake. He stirred me to help you.

SEBASTIAN What caused you to take my side? What is happening here? Am I insane or dreaming? Let me forget this. If this is a dream, let me stay asleep!

OLIVIA Please, come in. Listen to me.

SEBASTIAN Madam, I will accompany you.

OLIVIA Good. I'm glad you agree! *[The COUNTESS OLIVIA and SEBASTIAN depart.]*

ACT IV, SCENE 2

A room in Olivia's house.

[Enter MARIA and CLOWN]

MARIA Nay, I prithee, put on this gown and this beard; make him believe thou art Sir Topas the curate. Do it quickly; I'll call Sir Toby the whilst.
[Exit]

CLOWN Well, I'll put it on, and I will dissemble myself in't; and I would I were the first that ever dissembled in such a gown. I am not tall enough to become the function well, nor lean enough to be thought a good student; but to be said an honest man and a good housekeeper goes as fairly as to say a careful man and a great scholar. The competitors enter.
[Enter SIR TOBY and MARIA]

SIR TOBY Jove bless thee, Master Parson.

CLOWN Bonos dies, Sir Toby; for, as the old hermit of Prague, that never saw pen and ink, very wittily said to a niece of King Gorboduc, 'That that is, is'; so I, being Master Parson, am Master Parson; for, what is 'that' but that, and 'is' but is?

SIR TOBY To him, Sir Topas.

CLOWN What ho, I say! peace in this prison!

SIR TOBY The knave counterfeits well; a good knave.

MALVOLIO *[Within]* Who calls there?

CLOWN Sir Topas the curate, who comes to visit Malvolio the lunatic.

MALVOLIO Sir Topas, Sir Topas, good Sir Topas, go to my lady.

CLOWN Out, hyperbolical fiend! How vexest thou this man! Talkest thou nothing but of ladies?

SIR TOBY Well said, Master Parson.

MALVOLIO Sir Topas, never was man thus wronged. Good Sir Topas, do not think I am mad; they have laid me here in hideous darkness.

ACT IV, SCENE 2

A room in the residence of the Countess Olivia in Illyria east of Italy.

[MARIA and FESTE enter.]

MARIA Feste, dress in this robe and fake beard. Pretend you are the priest Sir Topaz. While you dress, I will summon Sir Toby. *[MARIA departs.]*

CLOWN I will put on the disguise and pretend to be a priest. I hope I am the first man to disguise himself in a holy man's robe. I am not tall enough to play a priest nor skinny enough to play a starving student. But I'm sincere and neat, which is as good as being cautious and scholarly. The jokers are coming. *[SIR TOBY and MARIA enter.]*

SIR TOBY Jupiter bless you, parson.

CLOWN Good day, Sir Toby. As the religious recluse at Prague who never saw writing said to King Gorboduc's niece, "Whatever is, exists." I, the parson, am the parson. What is "that" but "I," and what is "is" but "exist"?

SIR TOBY Visit Malvolio, Sir Topaz.

CLOWN Greetings! Peace to your prison cell!

SIR TOBY Feste pretends well. He's a good rascal.

MALVOLIO *[MALVOLIO in the dark room]* Who is calling me?

CLOWN I am the priest, Sir Topaz, come to visit Malvolio the madman.

MALVOLIO Oh, Sir Topaz, Sir Topaz, good priest, go to the Countess Olivia.

CLOWN Out, great demon! Why do you obsess Malvolio! Why does he talk only about women?

SIR TOBY Good question, parson.

MALVOLIO Sir Topaz, no man was ever so mistreated as I. Sir Topaz, I am not insane. These jokers have confined me to a dark room.

CLOWN Fie, thou dishonest Satan! I call thee by the most modest terms; for I am one of those gentle ones that will use the devil himself with courtesy. Sayest thou that house is dark?

MALVOLIO As hell, Sir Topas.

CLOWN Why, it hath bay windows transparent as barricadoes, and the clearstories towards the south north are as lustrous as ebony; and yet complainest thou of obstruction?

MALVOLIO I am not mad, Sir Topas; I say to you, this house is dark.

CLOWN Madman, thou errest. I say, there is no darkness but ignorance, in which thou are more puzzled than the Egyptians in their fog.

MALVOLIO I say, this house is as dark as ignorance, though ignorance were as dark as hell; and I say, there was never man thus abused. I am no more mad than you are. Make the trial of it in any constant question.

CLOWN What is the opinion of Pythagoras concerning wild fowl?

MALVOLIO That the soul of our grandam might haply inhabit a bird.

CLOWN What thinkest thou of his opinion?

MALVOLIO I think nobly of the soul, and no way approve his opinion.

CLOWN Fare thee well. Remain thou still in darkness. Thou shalt hold the opinion of Pythagoras ere I will allow of thy wits; and fear to kill a woodcock, lest thou dispossess the soul of thy grandam. Fare thee well.

MALVOLIO Sir Topas, Sir Topas!

SIR TOBY My most exquisite Sir Topas!

CLOWN Nay, I am for all waters.

MARIA Thou mightest have done this without thy beard and gown. He sees thee not.

CLOWN Shame, you lying demon. I call you modest names. I am so courteous that I respect Satan himself. Is this room dark?

MALVOLIO As dark as hell, Sir Topaz.

CLOWN It has large windows as clear as barricades. The upper panes in the south north are as bright as blackness. Why do you complain of darkness?

MALVOLIO I am not crazy, Sir Topaz. I declare that the room is dark.

CLOWN Maniac, you are wrong. You imagine darkness, which befuddles you like Egyptians in a fog.

MALVOLIO This room is as dark as ignorance, which is black as hell. No one was ever so mistreated. I am as sane as you. Test me with questions.

CLOWN What did Pythagoras the Greek philosopher think about wild birds?

MALVOLIO He said that a grandmother's soul might pass into the body of a bird.

CLOWN Do you agree with Pythagoras?

MALVOLIO I respect the soul, but disapprove of Pythagoras's belief.

CLOWN Good-bye. Stay in this dark room. I will not call you sane until you agree with Pythagoras. You will be afraid of killing a snipe, who might be the new body of your grandmother. Good-bye.

MALVOLIO Sir Topaz, come back!

SIR TOBY Well done, Sir Topaz!

CLOWN I swim in all waters.

MARIA You didn't need the fake beard and robe. Malvolio can't see you in the dark room.

SIR TOBY To him in thine own voice, and bring me word how thou findest him. I would we were well rid of this knavery. If he may be conveniently delivered, I would he were, for I am now so far in offence with my niece that I cannot pursue with any safety this sport to the upshot. Come by and by to my chamber. *[Exeunt SIR TOBY and MARIA]*

CLOWN *[Singing]* 'Hey, Robin, jolly Robin,
Tell me how thy lady does.'

MALVOLIO Fool!

CLOWN 'My lady is unkind, perdie.'

MALVOLIO Fool!

CLOWN 'Alas, why is she so?'

MALVOLIO Fool, I say!

CLOWN 'She loves another.' Who calls, ha?

MALVOLIO Good fool, as ever thou wilt deserve well at my hand, help me to a candle, and pen, ink, and paper. As I am a gentleman, I will live to be thankful to thee for't.

CLOWN Master Malvolio?

MALVOLIO Ay, good fool.

CLOWN Alas, sir, how fell you beside your five wits?

MALVOLIO Fool, there was never man so notoriously abused. I am as well in my wits, fool, as thou art.

CLOWN But as well? then you are mad indeed, if you be no better in your wits than a fool.

MALVOLIO They have here propertied me; keep me in darkness, send ministers to me, asses, and do all they can to face me out of my wits.

CLOWN Advise you what you say; the minister is here. Malvolio, Malvolio, thy wits the heavens restore! Endeavour thyself to sleep, and leave thy vain bibble babble.

MALVOLIO Sir Topas!

SIR TOBY Talk to him in a normal voice and tell me how he feels. I am eager to end this prank. If I could let him go free, I would. I have so insulted the Countess Olivia that I can't carry on this trick to the end. Come soon to my room. *[SIR TOBY and MARIA depart.]*

CLOWN *[FESTE sings in his own voice.] Hey, Robin, merry Robin, How is your girlfriend?*

MALVOLIO Jester!

CLOWN *By God, my girlfriend is unkind.*

MALVOLIO Jester!

CLOWN *Why is she unkind to you?*

MALVOLIO Feste the jester!

CLOWN *She loves somebody else.* Who is calling me?

MALVOLIO Feste, if I've ever been generous to you, give me a candle, pen, ink, and paper. On my honor, I will always be grateful to you.

CLOWN Is that you, Malvolio?

MALVOLIO Yes, good Feste.

CLOWN How did you lose your mind?

MALVOLIO Feste, no man has ever been so mistreated as I. I am as sane as you.

CLOWN As sane as I? Then you are crazy if you are as mad as a jester.

MALVOLIO They locked me up. They keep me in the dark, send idiotic ministers to me, and try to make me seem crazy.

CLOWN Think about what you just said. The minister is still here. *[In the voice of SIR TOPAZ.]* Malvolio, may God restore your sanity! Rest up and stop babbling.

MALVOLIO Sir Topaz!

CLOWN Maintain no words with him, good fellow.
Who, I, sir? not I, sir. God be wi' you, good Sir Topas. Marry, amen. I will, sir, I will.

MALVOLIO Fool, fool, fool, I say!

CLOWN Alas, sir, be patient. What say you, sir? I am shent for speaking to you.

MALVOLIO Good fool, help me to some light and some paper. I tell thee, I am as well in my wits as any man in Illyria.

CLOWN Well-a-day that you were, sir!

MALVOLIO By this hand, I am. Good fool, some ink, paper, and light; and convey what I will set down to my lady. It shall advantage thee more than ever the bearing of letter did.

CLOWN I will help you to't. But tell me true, are you not mad indeed? or do you but counterfeit?

MALVOLIO Believe me, I am not; I tell thee true.

CLOWN Nay, I'll ne'er believe a madman till I see his brains. I will fetch you light and paper and ink.

MALVOLIO Fool, I'll requite it in the highest degree. I prithee, be gone.

CLOWN *[Singing]* I am gone, sir.
And anon, sir,
I'll be with you again,
In a trice,
Like to the old Vice,
Your need to sustain;
Who, with dagger of lath,
In his rage and his wrath,
Cries, aha! to the devil:
Like a mad lad,
Pare thy nails, dad;
Adieu, goodman devil.
[Exit]

CLOWN *[In the voice of SIR TOPAZ.]* Don't talk to Malvolio, Feste. *[In the voice of FESTE.]* Me, sir? I won't, Sir Topaz. *[In the voice of SIR TOPAZ.]* So be it, Feste. *[In the voice of FESTE.]* I will do as you said, Sir Topaz.

MALVOLIO Feste, come back!

CLOWN Don't excite yourself. What do you want, Malvolio? Sir Topaz scolded me for talking to you.

MALVOLIO Please, Feste, give me a candle and paper. I promise you, I am as sane as anyone in Illyria.

CLOWN That's too bad, Malvolio!

MALVOLIO I swear I am sane. Please, Feste, I need ink, paper, and a candle. Then take my letter to the Countess Olivia. You will earn more than you ever have for delivering a letter.

CLOWN I will help you. Are you really sane? Or are you just pretending to be sane?

MALVOLIO Trust me, I am not pretending. I am telling the truth.

CLOWN I will never trust a maniac until I see inside his head. I will bring you a candle, paper, and ink.

MALVOLIO Feste, I will repay you fully. Please, hurry.

CLOWN *[FESTE singing.]* I leave you, Malvolio. I will be back soon. I'll come back in a jiffy to bring what you need. With a stick for a dagger, Sin displays his anger by crying "ha!" at Satan. Like a crazy boy, cut your claws, Satan. God be with you, good Satan. *[FESTE goes out.]*

ACT IV, SCENE 3

Olivia's garden.

[Enter SEBASTIAN]

SEBASTIAN
This is the air; that is the glorious sun;
This pearl she gave me, I do feel't and see't;
And though 'tis wonder that enwraps me thus,
Yet 'tis not madness. Where's Antonio, then?
I could not find him at the Elephant;
Yet there he was; and there I found this credit,
That he did range the town to seek me out.
His counsel now might do me golden service;
For though my soul disputes well with my sense,
That this may be some error, but no madness,
Yet doth this accident and flood of fortune
So far exceed all instance, all discourse,
That I am ready to distrust mine eyes,
And wrangle with my reason, that persuades me
To any other trust but that I am mad,
Or else the lady's mad; yet, if 'twere so,
She could not sway her house, command her followers,
Take and give back affairs and their dispatch
With such a smooth, discreet, and stable bearing
As I perceive she does. There's something in't
That is deceivable. But here the lady comes.
[Enter OLIVIA and PRIEST]

OLIVIA
Blame not this haste of mine. If you mean well,
Now go with me and with this holy man
Into the chantry by. There, before him,
And underneath that consecrated roof,
Plight me the full assurance of your faith,
That my most jealous and too doubtful soul
May live at peace. He shall conceal it
Whiles you are willing it shall come to note,
What time we will our celebration keep
According to my birth. What do you say?

SEBASTIAN
I'll follow this good man, and go with you;
And, having sworn truth, ever will be true.

OLIVIA
Then lead the way, good father; and heavens so shine,
That they may fairly note this act of mine!
[Exeunt]

ACT IV, SCENE 3

The Countess Olivia's garden.

[SEBASTIAN enters.]

SEBASTIAN This is the air; that is the glorious sun; I hold and look at the pearl the Countess gave me. I can't make sense of it all, but I'm not crazy. Where did Antonio go? He didn't meet me at the Elephant. But he was there earlier. People said that he wandered the town looking for me. I need his advice now. My mind doubts my good sense. This generosity may be an error, but it is not lunacy. This outpouring of good luck is far more than I have ever experienced or heard of. I distrust what I see. I debate with myself. I conclude that either I am crazy or the Countess Olivia is. If she were insane, however, she could not rule a household, command a staff, or conduct business with such a calm, unruffled expression as she does. Something is wrong. Here comes the Countess. *[OLIVIA enters with a priest.]*

OLIVIA Don't blame me for being in a rush. If you are sincere, go with me and the priest into the nearby chapel. Before him and in a holy place, pledge your vow. Then my spirit will give up its suspicions and doubts. The priest will hide your pledge from the public until you want to announce it. Then we will have a public celebration suited to a countess. Do you agree?

SEBASTIAN I will follow this priest and enter the chapel with you. When I pledge myself to you, I will be loyal.

OLIVIA Lead the way, good priest, and let heaven shine on my choice of mate! *[OLIVIA, SEBASTIAN, and the priest go out.]*

ACT V, SCENE 1

The street before Olivia's house.

[Enter CLOWN and FABIAN]

FABIAN Now, as thou lovest me, let me see his letter.

CLOWN Good master Fabian, grant me another request.

FABIAN Anything.

CLOWN Do not desire to see this letter.

FABIAN This is, to give a dog, and in recompense desire my dog again.

[Enter DUKE, VIOLA, CURIO, and LORDS]

DUKE Belong you to the Lady Olivia, friends?

CLOWN Ay, sir, we are some of her trappings.

DUKE I know thee well. How dost thou, my good fellow?

CLOWN Truly, sir, the better for my foes and the worse for my friends.

DUKE Just the contrary, the better for thy friends.

CLOWN No, sir, the worse.

DUKE How can that be?

CLOWN Marry, sir, they praise me and make an ass of me; now my foes tell me plainly I am an ass: so that by my foes, sir, I profit in the knowledge of myself, and by my friends I am abused: so that, conclusions to be as kisses, if your four negatives make your two affirmatives, why then, the worse for my friends and the better for my foes.

DUKE Why, this is excellent.

CLOWN By my troth, sir, no, though it please you to be one of my friends.

DUKE Thou shalt not be the worse for me. There's gold.

CLOWN But that it would be double-dealing, sir, I would you could make it another.

DUKE Oh, you give me ill counsel.

ACT V, SCENE 1

The street in front of the residence of the Countess Olivia in Illyria east of Italy.

[FESTE and FABIAN enter.]

FABIAN	If you are my friend, show me Malvolio's letter to the Countess.
CLOWN	Fabian, promise me something.
FABIAN	Anything.
CLOWN	Don't ask for this letter.
FABIAN	That's the same as giving me a dog and demanding it back again as payment. *[DUKE ORSINO, VIOLA disguised as CESARIO, CURIO, and LORDS enter.]*
DUKE	Are you the Countess Olivia's staff?
CLOWN	Yes, we wear her uniform.
DUKE	I recognize you. How are you, Feste?
CLOWN	Indeed, sir, I profit from my enemies and suffer my friends.
DUKE	Don't you mean that you profit from friends?
CLOWN	No, sir, I suffer from them.
DUKE	Why is that?
CLOWN	My friends flatter me and ridicule me. Enemies call me a fool straight out. From my enemies, I learn more about myself. My friends only deceive me. My conclusions are like kisses. If four noes make two yeses, then I profit from my enemies and suffer my friends.
DUKE	A good joke, Feste.
CLOWN	No, sir, even though you are a friend.
DUKE	I won't harm you. Here's a gold coin.
CLOWN	If it weren't dishonest, I would like two coins.
DUKE	You give me bad advice.

CLOWN Put your grace in your pocket, sir, for this once, and let your flesh and blood obey it.

DUKE Well, I will be so much a sinner, to be a double-dealer; there's another.

CLOWN Primo, secundo, tertio, is a good play; and the old saying is, the third pays for all. The triplex, sir, is a good tripping measure; or the bells of Saint Bennet, sir, may put you in mind; one, two, three.

DUKE You can fool no more money out of me at this throw. If you will let your lady know I am here to speak with her, and bring her along with you, it may awake my bounty further.

CLOWN Marry, sir, lullaby to your bounty till I come again. I go, sir, but I would not have you to think that my desire of having is the sin of covetousness; but, as you say, sir, let your bounty take a nap, I will awake it anon.
[Exit]

VIOLA Here comes the man, sir, that did rescue me.
[Enter ANTONIO and OFFICERS]

DUKE
That face of his I do remember well;
Yet, when I saw it last it was besmear'd
As black as Vulcan in the smoke of war.
A bawbling vessel was he captain of,
For shallow draught and bulk unprizable,
With which such scathful grapple did he make
With the most noble bottom of our fleet,
That very envy and the tongue of loss
Cried fame and honour on him. What's the matter?

FIRST OFFICER
Orsino, this is that Antonio
That took the Phoenix and her fraught from Candy;
And this is he that did the Tiger board,
When your young nephew Titus lost his leg.
Here in the streets, desperate of shame and state,
In private brabble did we apprehend him.

VIOLA
He did me kindness, sir, drew on my side;
But in conclusion put strange speech upon me,
I know not what 'twas but distraction.

CLOWN Put virtue in your pocket. Just this once, let your hand be generous.

DUKE If I were a sinner, I would be a trickster. Here's another coin.

CLOWN First, second, third is a good roll of the dice. The old wisdom is that the third throw wins. Triple time is good for dancing. The church bells of Saint Benedict may make you think one, two, three.

DUKE You won't get a third coin out of me. If you will summon the Countess and bring her here, I may be more generous.

CLOWN Sing gently to your generosity until I return. Don't think that my greed is one of the seven deadly sins. Let your generosity rest until I awaken it again. *[FESTE goes out.]*

VIOLA Here is the man, Duke Orsino, who rescued me. *[ANTONIO enters with police officers.]*

DUKE I remember his face. The last time I saw him, he was covered in the soot of war. He captained a paltry ship, shallow and worthless. He threw a grappling hook so hard against the bottoms of my fleet that he won fame for his feat. Why is he under arrest?

FIRST OFFICER Duke Orsino, this is Antonio, who stole the *Phoenix* and her cargo from the island of Crete. He boarded the *Tiger* when your nephew Titus lost his leg. We arrested this notorious man here in a street brawl.

VIOLA He did me a favor, sir, by fighting for me. He spoke strangely to me as though he were crazy.

DUKE
Notable pirate! thou salt-water thief!
What foolish boldness brought thee to their mercies,
Whom thou, in terms so bloody and so dear,
Hast made thine enemies?

ANTONIO
Orsino, noble sir,
Be pleased that I shake off these names you give me.
Antonio never yet was thief or pirate,
Though I confess, on base and ground enough,
Orsino's enemy. A witchcraft drew me hither.
That most ingrateful boy there by your side,
From the rude sea's enraged and foamy mouth
Did I redeem; a wreck past hope he was.
His life I gave him and did thereto add
My love, without retention or restraint,
All his in dedication; for his sake
Did I expose myself, pure for his love,
Into the danger of this adverse town;
Drew to defend him when he was beset:
Where being apprehended, his false cunning,
Not meaning to partake with me in danger,
Taught him to face me out of his acquaintance,
And grew a twenty years removed thing
While one could wink; denied me mine own purse,
Which I had recommended to his use
Not half an hour before.

VIOLA
How can this be?

DUKE
When came he to this town?

ANTONIO
To-day, my lord; and for three months before,
No interim, not a minute's vacancy,
Both day and night did we keep company.
[Enter OLIVIA and Attendants]

DUKE
Here comes the countess; now heaven walks on earth.
But for thee, fellow,—fellow, thy words are madness.
Three months this youth hath tended upon me;
But more of that anon. Take him aside.

OLIVIA
What would my lord, but that he may not have,
Wherein Olivia may seem serviceable?
Cesario, you do not keep promise with me.

VIOLA
Madam!

DUKE
Gracious Olivia—

DUKE Famous pirate! Ocean plunderer! What foolishness made you risk arrest? What enemies did you risk your blood for by fighting in the street?

ANTONIO Duke Orsino, I am pleased to refute these names you call me. I was never a thief or a pirate. I had reason to attack your ships. Bedazzlement drew me here. I saved this ungrateful boy at your side from drowning. He was a mess. I offered him my friendship and loyalty as well as his life. For him, I risked capture in your town. I drew my sword to defend him from enemies. When the police seized me, the boy refused to come to my aid and pretended he didn't know me. As quick as a wink, he removed himself from me. He refused to give me the wallet that I had entrusted to him only thirty minutes before.

VIOLA This is untrue.

DUKE When did he arrive here?

ANTONIO Today, sir. He has lived with me for three months, day and night.

[The COUNTESS OLIVIA enters with her staff.]

DUKE Here comes the Countess Olivia, who brings heaven to earth. You spoil the day, Antonio. Your words are insane. For three months, Cesario has been my aide. We'll discuss that later. Take him away.

OLIVIA How can I serve you, except to give you my love? Cesario, you have violated your vow.

VIOLA Madam!

DUKE Gracious Olivia—

OLIVIA What do you say, Cesario? Good my lord,

VIOLA My lord would speak; my duty hushes me.

OLIVIA If it be aught to the old tune, my lord,
It is as fat and fulsome to mine ear
As howling after music.

DUKE Still so cruel?

OLIVIA Still so constant, lord.

DUKE What, to perverseness? you uncivil lady,
To whose ingrate and unauspicious altars
My soul the faithfull'st offerings hath breathed out
That e'er devotion tender'd! What shall I do?

OLIVIA Even what it please my lord, that shall become him.

DUKE Why should I not, had I the heart to do it,
Like to the Egyptian thief at point of death,
Kill what I love?—a savage jealousy
That sometimes savours nobly. But hear me this:
Since you to non-regardance cast my faith,
And that I partly know the instrument
That screws me from my true place in your favour,
Live you the marble-breasted tyrant still;
But this your minion, whom I know you love,
And whom, by heaven I swear, I tender dearly,
Him will I tear out of that cruel eye,
Where he sits crowned in his master's spite.
Come, boy, with me; my thoughts are ripe in mischief.
I'll sacrifice the lamb that I do love,
To spite a raven's heart within a dove.

VIOLA And I, most jocund, apt, and willingly,
To do you rest, a thousand deaths would die.

OLIVIA Where goes Cesario?

VIOLA After him I love
More than I love these eyes, more than my life,
More, by all mores, than e'er I shall love wife.
If I do feign, you witnesses above
Punish my life for tainting of my love!

OLIVIA Ay me, detested! how am I beguiled!

VIOLA Who does beguile you? who does do you wrong?

OLIVIA	Answer me, Cesario! Good sir—
VIOLA	The Duke is speaking. I must be silent.
OLIVIA	If he sings the same old tune, Cesario, it is as nauseating as howling to music.
DUKE	Are you still cruel to me?
OLIVIA	I am the same, Duke.
DUKE	Are you being stubborn? You are rude to me, who has made sweet offerings on your ungrateful, unlucky altars. What do you want me to do?
OLIVIA	Whatever will please you.
DUKE	Why shouldn't I, like the Egyptian pirate, kill you, if I had the heart to do it? Savage jealousy sometimes seems noble. Listen to me: Since you toss me away and I suspect the fellow who takes my place in your heart, you may live with your hard-hearted cruelty. But this lad whom you love, and whom I hold in my affection, I will rip him out of your eye, where he flourishes, despite his master's suffering. Come with me, Cesario. I am bristling with anger. I will sacrifice a favorite lamb to punish a black heart within an innocent breast.
VIOLA	I would willingly, cheerfully die a thousand deaths to comfort you.
OLIVIA	What do you mean, Cesario?
VIOLA	I love Duke Orsino more than my eyes, my life, more than any woman I could marry. If I lie, you witnesses may kill me for discrediting my affection.
OLIVIA	Oh, me, how detestable! I have been deceived!
VIOLA	Who tricks you? Who wrongs you?

OLIVIA Hast thou forgot thyself? Is it so long?
Call forth the holy father.

DUKE Come, away!

OLIVIA Whither, my lord? Cesario, husband, stay.

DUKE Husband!

OLIVIA
Ay, husband: can he that deny?

DUKE Her husband, sirrah!

VIOLA No, my lord, not I.

OLIVIA Alas, it is the baseness of thy fear
That makes thee strangle thy propriety.
Fear not, Cesario; take thy fortunes up;
Be that thou know'st thou art, and then thou art
As great as that thou fear'st.
[Enter PRIEST]
Oh, welcome, father!
Father, I charge thee, by thy reverence,
Here to unfold, though lately we intended
To keep in darkness what occasion now
Reveals before 'tis ripe, what thou dost know
Hath newly pass'd between this youth and me.

PRIEST A contract of eternal bond of love,
Confirm'd by mutual joinder of your hands,
Attested by the holy close of lips,
Strengthen'd by interchangement of your rings;
And all the ceremony of this compact
Seal'd in my function, by my testimony:
Since when, my watch hath told me, toward my grave
I have trevell'd but two hours.

DUKE O thou dissembling cub! what wilt thou be
When time hath sow'd a grizzle on thy case?
Or will not else thy craft so quickly grow,
That thine own trip shall be thine overthrow?
Farewell, and take her; but direct thy feet
Where thou and I henceforth may never meet.

VIOLA My lord, I do protest.

OLIVIA Oh, do not swear!
Hold little faith, though thou hast too much fear.
[Enter SIR ANDREW]

OLIVIA Have you forgotten already? In so short a time? Call the priest.

DUKE Come, Cesario!

OLIVIA Where are you going, Cesario? My husband, stay with me.

DUKE Husband!

OLIVIA Yes, he is my husband. Can he deny it?

DUKE Sir, you married the Countess!

VIOLA No, lord, I didn't.

OLIVIA You lie about your vows because you are afraid of the Duke. Don't be afraid, Cesario. Accept your change of status. If you claim to be husband to a countess, you are an equal of a duke. *[The PRIEST enters.]* Welcome, Father! Father, I demand that you reveal the wedding. We intended to have a secret marriage until it was time to announce it. Reveal what has happened between Cesario and me.

PRIEST I performed an eternal marriage. Affirmed by the joining of hands. Sworn by your vows. Proven by the exchange of wedding rings. This union I sealed under my office as priest. The marriage, according to my watch, was only two hours ago.

DUKE Cesario, you lying pup! Will you be worse by the time you grow a beard? Will your sneaking become so bad that you trap yourself? Good-bye, and take the Countess with you. Don't ever cross my path again.

VIOLA Duke Orsino, you are wrong.

OLIVIA Don't swear to a lie, Cesario! Keep your honesty, even though you are afraid of the Duke. *[SIR ANDREW enters.]*

SIR ANDREW For the love of God, a surgeon! Send one presently to Sir Toby.

OLIVIA What's the matter?

SIR ANDREW He has broke my head across and has given Sir Toby a bloody coxcomb too. For the love of God, your help! I had rather than forty pound I were at home.

OLIVIA Who has done this, Sir Andrew?

SIR ANDREW The count's gentleman, one Cesario. We took him for a coward, but he's the very devil incardinate.

DUKE My gentleman, Cesario?

SIR ANDREW 'Od's lifelings! Here he is! You broke my head for nothing; and that that I did, I was set on to do't by Sir Toby.

VIOLA Why do you speak to me? I never hurt you:
You drew your sword upon me without cause;
But I bespake you fair, and hurt you not.

SIR ANDREW If a bloody coxcomb be a hurt, you have hurt me. I think you set nothing by a bloody coxcomb. *[Enter SIR TOBY and CLOWN]* Here comes Sir Toby halting; you shall hear more: but if he had not been in drink, he would have tickled you other-gates than he did.

DUKE How now, gentleman! how is't with you?

SIR TOBY That's all one; Has hurt me, and there's the end on't. Sot. didst see Dick surgeon, Sot?

CLOWN Oh, he's drunk, Sir Toby, an hour agone; his eyes were set at eight i' the morning.

SIR TOBY Then he's a rogue, and a passy measures pavin. I hate a drunken rogue.

OLIVIA Away with him! Who hath made this havoc with them?

SIR ANDREW I'll help you, Sir Toby, because we'll be dressed together.

SIR TOBY Will you help? an ass-head and a coxcomb and a knave, a thin-faced knave, a gull!

OLIVIA Get him to bed, and let his hurt be looked to.
[Exeunt CLOWN, FABIAN, SIR TOBY, and SIR ANDREW]
[Enter SEBASTIAN]

SIR ANDREW Call a doctor! Send help to Sir Toby.

OLIVIA What happened?

SIR ANDREW He broke my skull and bloodied Sir Toby. For God's sake, help us! I would give eighty dollars to be at home.

OLIVIA Who hurt you, Sir Andrew?

SIR ANDREW It was Cesario, the Duke's ambassador. We thought he was a coward, but he's a bloody demon.

DUKE Are you accusing my aide, Cesario?

SIR ANDREW God's little lives! Here is Cesario! You cracked my skull for no reason. All I did was follow Sir Toby's orders.

VIOLA Why do you accuse me? I haven't hit you. You drew your weapon on me without provocation. But I was courteous to you and did you no harm.

SIR ANDREW If a bloody scalp be a harm, you have harmed me. I think you care nothing about hitting me in the head. *[SIR TOBY and FESTE enter.]* Here comes Sir Toby limping. You will hear more accusations. If Sir Toby had not been drunk, he would have retaliated better than he did.

DUKE How are you, Sir Toby! Are you hurt?

SIR TOBY It doesn't matter. Cesario wounded me. That's the whole truth. Idiot, did you find Doctor Dick, fool?

CLOWN He's been drunk for an hour, Sir Toby. His eyes haven't changed since 8:00 A.M.

SIR TOBY Then he's a rascal and an eight-bar dance. I despise a drunken scoundrel.

OLIVIA Take Sir Toby away! Who attacked Sir Andrew and Sir Toby?

SIR ANDREW I will aid you, Sir Toby. We will both have our wounds bandaged.

SIR TOBY How will you help? You're an ass's head, a twit, a rascal, a thin-cheeked felon, a dupe!

OLIVIA Put Sir Toby to bed and tend his wound. *[FESTE, FABIAN, SIR TOBY, and SIR ANDREW depart.]*
[SEBASTIAN enters.]

SEBASTIAN I am sorry, madam, I have hurt your kinsman;
But, had it been the brother of my blood,
I must have done no less with wit and safety.
You throw a strange regard upon me, and by that
I do perceive it hath offended you.
Pardon me, sweet one, even for the vows
We made each other but so late ago.

DUKE One face, one voice, one habit, and two persons,
A natural perspective, that is, and is not!

SEBASTIAN Antonio, O my dear Antonio!
How have the hours rack'd and tortured me
Since I have lost thee!

ANTONIO Sebastian are you?

SEBASTIAN Fear'st thou that, Antonio?

ANTONIO How have you made division of yourself?
An apple, cleft in two, is not more twin
Than these two creatures. Which is Sebastian?

OLIVIA Most wonderful!

SEBASTIAN Do I stand there? I never had a brother;
Nor can there he that deity in my nature,
Of here and everywhere. I had a sister,
Whom the blind waves and surges have devour'd.
Of charity, what kin are you to me?
What countryman? what name? what parentage?

VIOLA Of Messaline. Sebastian was my father;
Such a Sebastian was my brother too,
So went he suited to his watery tomb.
If spirits can assume both form and suit,
You come to fright us.

SEBASTIAN A spirit I am indeed;
But am in that dimension grossly clad
Which from the womb I did participate.
Were you a woman, as the rest goes even,
I should my tears let fall upon your cheek,
And say, "Thrice-welcome, drowned Viola!"

VIOLA My father had a mole upon his brow.

SEBASTIAN I apologize, madam, I have wounded your uncle Toby. Even if he had been my own brother, I could not avoid fighting back. You stare at me. I think I have offended you. Forgive me, sweetheart. We have only recently exchanged vows.

DUKE The same face, voice, garments, but two people who look alike. This is and is not possible!

SEBASTIAN Antonio, my dear friend! I have worried for hours since I was separated from you!

ANTONIO Are you Sebastian?

SEBASTIAN You don't believe it, Antonio?

ANTONIO Have you duplicated yourself? An apple cut in half is not more similar than these two people. Which is the real Sebastian?

OLIVIA A miracle!

SEBASTIAN Is that me? I don't have a brother. I can't be in two places at once. I had a sister Viola who drowned in the sea. Tell me, are you a relative? Who are you? What is your name? Who are your parents?

VIOLA My father Sebastian came from Messaline. I had a brother Sebastian, too. He drowned in the ocean. If you are a ghost, you have come in his body and clothing to scare us.

SEBASTIAN I am a spirit. I wear the body that I was born with. If you were female, I would weep and welcome you as my drowned sister Viola!

VIOLA My father had a mole on his forehead.

SEBASTIAN And so had mine.

VIOLA And died that day when Viola from her birth
Had number'd thirteen years.

SEBASTIAN Oh, that record is lively in my soul!
He finished indeed his mortal act
That day that made my sister thirteen years.

VIOLA If nothing lets to make us happy both
But this my masculine usurp'd attire,
Do not embrace me till each circumstance
Of place, time, fortune, do cohere and jump
That I am Viola; which to confirm,
I'll bring you a captain in this town,
Where lie my maiden weeds; by whose gentle help
I was preserved to serve this noble count.
All the occurrence of my fortune since
Hath been between this lady and this lord.

SEBASTIAN *[To OLIVIA]* So comes it, lady, you have been mistook;
But nature to her bias drew in that.
You would have been contracted to a maid;
Nor are you therein, by my life, deceived;
You are betroth'd both to a maid and man.

DUKE Be not amazed; right noble is his blood.
If this be so, as yet the glass seems true,
I shall have share in his most happy wreck.
[To VIOLA] Boy, thou hast said to me a thousand times
Thou never shouldst love woman like to me.

VIOLA And all those sayings will I over-swear;
And all those swearings keep as true in soul
As doth that orbed continent the fire
That severs day from night.

DUKE Give me thy hand;
And let me see thee in thy woman's weeds.

VIOLA The captain that did bring me first on shore
Hath my maid's garments. He upon some action
Is now in durance, at Malvolio's suit,
A gentleman, and follower of my lady's.

SEBASTIAN Mine, too.

VIOLA And died on my thirteenth birthday.

SEBASTIAN Oh, I remember the day! His last day was my sister's thirteenth birthday.

VIOLA My masculine disguise keeps us from reuniting. Don't embrace me until I can be Viola again. I will take you to the home of a sea captain who keeps my female garments. He helped me join the staff of Duke Orsino. My job has been to serve as the Duke's ambassador to the Countess Olivia.

SEBASTIAN *[SEBASTIAN to his wife OLIVIA]* It turns out, lady, that you are mistaken. But nature led you to me. You may have courted a girl. But you are not tricked. You love twins, a girl and a man.

DUKE Don't be puzzled. Sebastian has noble blood. If the mirror is true, I will court his sister. *[DUKE ORSINO to VIOLA disguised as CESARIO.]* Cesario, you have told me a thousand times that you could never love a woman as you love me.

VIOLA I will vow those statements again. My oaths were as true as the sun, which divides day and night.

DUKE Give me your hand. I want to see you in female garments.

VIOLA The captain who rescued me has my clothing. He is in jail because of Malvolio's charge.

OLIVIA He shall enlarge him. Fetch Malvolio hither;
And yet, alas, now I remember me,
They say, poor gentleman, he's much distract.
[Re-enter CLOWN with a letter, and FABIAN]
A most extracting frenzy of mine own
From my remembrance clearly banish'd his.
How does he, sirrah?

CLOWN Truly, madam, he holds Beelzebub at the stave's end as well as a man in his case may do: has here writ a letter to you; I should have given 't to you to-day morning, but as a madman's epistles are no gospels, so it skills not much when they are delivered.

OLIVIA Open't, and read it.

CLOWN Look then to be well edified when the fool delivers the madman. *[Reads]* 'By the Lord, madam'—

OLIVIA How now! art thou mad?

CLOWN No, madam, I do but read madness; an your ladyship will have it as it ought to be, you must allow Vox.

OLIVIA Prithee, read i' thy right wits.

CLOWN So I do, madonna; but to read his right wits is to read thus: therefore perpend, my princess, and give ear.

OLIVIA Read it you, sirrah. *[To FABIAN]*

FABIAN *[Reads]* 'By the Lord, madam, you wrong me, and the world shall know it. Though you have put me into darkness and given your drunken cousin rule over me, yet have I the benefit of my senses as well as your ladyship. I have your own letter that induced me to the semblance I put on; with the which I doubt not but to do myself much right, or you much shame. Think of me as you please. I leave my duty a little unthought of, and speak out of my injury.

The madly-used Malvolio.'

OLIVIA Did he write this?

CLOWN Ay, madam.

DUKE This savours not much of distraction.

OLIVIA Malvolio will free him. Bring Malvolio here. But, I just remembered that Malvolio is insane. *[FESTE returns with a letter, accompanied by FABIAN.]* This furor made me forget his insanity. How is Malvolio, Feste?

CLOWN He holds Satan at the end of a stick as well as anybody could. Malvolio wrote this letter to you. I should have delivered it this morning. But since the letters of lunatics are worthless, it doesn't matter if they are delivered.

OLIVIA Open and read it.

CLOWN Expect to be educated when a jester speaks the words of a lunatic. *[FESTE reads MALVOLIO's letter.]* "By God, Madam"—

OLIVIA What, are you crazy?

CLOWN I'm sane. The letter is crazy. If you want a sane statement, you must let Malvolio speak for himself.

OLIVIA Read it straight.

CLOWN I am, my lady. To read him as a sane man, I must continue. Listen carefully, my princess.

OLIVIA You read it, sir. *[She speaks to FABIAN.]*

FABIAN *[FABIAN reads MALVOLIO's letter.]* "By the Lord, madam, I will tell everybody that you have wronged me. You have imprisoned me in a dark room and let your drunken kinsman Toby control me. But I am as sane as you, Countess. I have a letter from you that bid me dress like this. With your letter, I hope to exonerate myself and shame you. Think what you will of me. I speak not like a servant, but like a victim. The mistreated Malvolio."

OLIVIA Did Malvolio write this?

CLOWN Yes, ma'am.

DUKE This doesn't sound like lunacy.

OLIVIA See him deliver'd, Fabian; bring him hither.
[Exit FABIAN]
My lord, so please you, these things further thought on,
To think me as well a sister as a wife,
One day shall crown the alliance on't, so please you,
Here at my house and at my proper cost.

DUKE Madam, I am most apt to embrace your offer.
[To VIOLA] Your master quits you; and for your service done him,
So much against the mettle of your sex,
So far beneath your soft and tender breeding,
And since you call'd me master for so long,
Here is my hand. You shall from this time be
Your master's mistress.

OLIVIA A sister! you are she.
[Re-enter FABIAN with MALVOLIO]

DUKE Is this the madman?

OLIVIA Ay, my lord, the same.
How now, Malvolio?

MALVOLIO Madam, you have done me wrong,
Notorious wrong.

OLIVIA Have I, Malvolio? no.

MALVOLIO Lady, you have. Pray you, peruse that letter.
You must not now deny it is your hand.
Write from it, if you can, in hand or phrase;
Or say 'tis not your seal, not your invention.
You can say none of this; well, grant it then,
And tell me, in the modesty of honour,
Why you have given me such clear lights of favour,
Bade me come smiling and cross-garter'd to you,
To put on yellow stockings and to frown
Upon Sir Toby and the lighter people;
And, acting this in an obedient hope,
Why have you suffer'd me to be imprison'd,
Kept in a dark house, visited by the priest,
And made the most notorious geck and gull
That e'er invention play'd on? tell me why.

OLIVIA Set him free, Fabian. Bring him here. *[FABIAN goes out.]* Duke Orsino, if you agree, I will be your sister-in-law and Sebastian's wife. I will pay for a double wedding at my house.

DUKE Madam, I accept your offer. *[To VIOLA disguised as CESARIO.]* Your master gives you up. You have served him well. Unlike a woman and far from your aristocratic upbringing. Since you have called me master for three months, I propose marriage to you. From now on, you are mistress to your master.

OLIVIA You are now my sister-in-law! *[FABIAN returns with MALVOLIO.]*

DUKE Is this the lunatic?

OLIVIA Yes, my lord. How are you feeling, Malvolio?

MALVOLIO Madam, you have treated me terribly.

OLIVIA Have I, Malvolio? I disagree.

MALVOLIO Countess, you have. Please, read this letter. You must agree that this is your handwriting. Copy any phrase you wish. Say it is not your seal or your composition. You can't deny it. Admit it and tell me honorably, why did you pretend to love me? You asked me to come to you in cross-tied garters and a smile. You asked me to wear yellow hose, to frown at Sir Toby and your staff. I obeyed you. Why did you have me locked up? Why was I kept in darkness and visited by a priest? Why was I treated like a simpleton and fool? Give me a reason.

OLIVIA Alas, Malvolio, this is not my writing,
Though, I confess, much like the character;
But out of question 'tis Maria's hand.
And now I do bethink me, it was she
First told me thou wast mad; then camest in smiling,
And in such forms which here were presupposed
Upon thee in the letter. Prithee, be content.
This practice hath most shrewdly pass'd upon thee;
But when we know the grounds and authors of it,
Thou shalt be both the plaintiff and the judge
Of thine own cause.

FABIAN Good madam, hear me speak.
And let no quarrel nor no brawl to come
Taint the condition of this present hour,
Which I have wonder'd at. In hope it shall not,
Most freely I confess, myself and Toby
Set this device against Malvolio here,
Upon some stubborn and uncourteous parts
We had conceived against him. Maria writ
The letter at Sir Toby's great importance;
In recompense whereof he hath married her.
How with a sportful malice it was follow'd,
May rather pluck on laughter than revenge,
If that the injuries be justly weigh'd
That have on both sides pass'd.

OLIVIA Alas, poor fool, how have they baffled thee!

CLOWN Why, 'some are born great, some achieve greatness,
and some have greatness thrown upon them.' I was
one, sir, in this interlude, one Sir Topas, sir; but
that's all one. 'By the Lord, fool, I am not mad!'
But do you remember? 'Madam, why laugh you at
such a barren rascal? An you smile not, he's gagged.'
And thus the whirligig of Time brings in his revenges.

MALVOLIO I'll be revenged on the whole pack of you.
[Exit]

OLIVIA He hath been most notoriously abused.

DUKE Pursue him, and entreat him to a peace.
He hath not told us of the captain yet.

OLIVIA Malvolio, I didn't write this letter. It looks like my handwriting. It is obviously Maria's handwriting. I remember that she informed me that you were insane. You arrived smiling in the costume dictated by the letter. Please, don't be angry. You have been cleverly tricked. But we know who did it and why. You may pass judgment on the jokers.

FABIAN Madam, let me speak. Let no argument or fight destroy the happiness of this hour. I have admired this reunion. To preserve your happiness, I confess that Toby and I plotted against Malvolio. We insulted him because of his stubbornness and discourtesy to us. At Sir Toby's direction, Maria wrote the letter. As her reward, Sir Toby wed Maria. The wedding concluded this funny trick. It was meant to be humorous, not harmful. The harm on both sides balance.

OLIVIA Poor Malvolio, how they have befuddled you!

CLOWN "Some people are great at birth, some make themselves great, and some find advancement by accident." In this plot, I played Sir Topaz, Malvolio. But it doesn't matter now. "By the Lord, Feste, I am not insane." Do you remember saying that? "Countess, why do you laugh at such an empty-headed rogue? Unless you laugh at his joke, he can't speak." Time turns the tables and brings vengeance.

MALVOLIO I will punish all four of you. *[MALVOLIO goes out.]*

OLIVIA He is terribly hurt.

DUKE Follow him and soothe his injury. Malvolio hasn't explained why the captain is in jail.

When that is known and golden time convents,
A solemn combination shall be made
Of our dear souls. Meantime, sweet sister,
We will not part from hence. Cesario, come;
For so you shall be, while you are a man;
But when in other habits you are seen,
Orsino's mistress and his fancy queen.
[Exeunt all, but CLOWN]

CLOWN *[Sings]*

When that I was and a little tiny boy,
With hey, ho, the wind and the rain,
A foolish thing was but a toy,
For the rain it raineth every day.
But when I came to man's estate,
With hey, ho, the wind and the rain,
'Gainst knaves and thieves men shut their gate,
For the rain it raineth every day.
But when I came, alas! to wive,
With hey, ho, the wind and the rain,
By swaggering could I never thrive,
For the rain it raineth every day.
But when I came unto my beds,
With hey, ho, the wind and the rain,
With tosspots still had drunken heads,
For the rain it raineth every day.
A great while ago the world begun,
With hey, ho, the wind and the rain,
But that's all one, our play is done,
And we'll strive to please you every day.
[Exit]

When we work that out, in time, we will solemnize our marriage. Meanwhile, sweet Olivia, we will not leave you. Cesario, come with me. In men's clothing, you are still Cesario. In women's clothes, you will be Duke Orsino's mistress and queen.
[Everyone departs except FESTE.]

CLOWN *[FESTE sings.]* When I was a small boy, I remember the wind and rain, A toy was an amusement because it rained every day. When I grew to manhood, I remember the wind and rain, People shut their doors on rascals and thieves because it rained every day. But when I married, I remember the wind and rain, I couldn't flourish because it rained every day. When I became an old man, I remember the wind and rain. Drunks still had hangovers because it rained every day. The world was created long ago, I remember the wind and rain. It doesn't matter. The play is finished. We actors will try to entertain you every day.
[FESTE goes out.]

Questions for Reflection

1. Contrast the unrequited loves of these couples from the play:

   - Duke Orsino/Countess Olivia
   - Countess Olivia/Cesario
   - Sir Andrew/Countess Olivia
   - Viola (Cesario)/Duke Orsino
   - the speaker and the "fair cruel maid" in "Come Away Death"

   Why were mix-ups and gender switches pleasing to Elizabethan audiences?

2. List the location and details of the shipwreck, including a double rescue and a floating mast. What do Antonio and the captain provide the rescued twins? How long have the twins been fatherless? Why does Shakespeare stress their vulnerability?

3. Cite lines from the play that stress the similarities between Viola and Cesario, her alter ego. What advantages does she enjoy in disguise as a male? What challenges does the dual role pose to the actor? makeup expert? costumer? other actors?

4. Contrast Duke Orsino, Cesario, and Sebastian as potential husbands for the Countess Olivia. Why does Sebastian agree so quickly to marry? Which male is more influenced by infatuation? by true love? by good luck? Why does Sebastian have reason to apologize to his bride for wounding Sir Toby's head?

5. Describe Malvolio's relationships with Feste, Maria, Sir Andrew, Sir Toby, Fabian, Sir Topas, the captain, and the Countess Olivia. What idiosyncrasies make Malvolio a likely butt of pranks and criticism? Why does Shakespeare leave unsettled Malvolio's vengeance and his punishment?

6. Discuss the use of songs in the play. What is the significance of Feste's old-fashioned love song "Come Away Death," drinking rounds shared with Fabian, Sir Andrew, and Sir Toby, and the realistic plaint that ends Act V?

7. Compose an extended definition of wit as displayed by Feste/Sir Topas, Viola, Sir Toby, and Sir Andrew. How does Sir Topas's wit contrast with the straightforward piety of the priest who conducts Olivia's marriage to Sebastian?

8. Discuss Shakespeare's presentation of grief. Why do Olivia and the twins have reasons for sadness? In what way does the loss of fathers enhance their need for emotional outlets?

9. Discuss the need of men like Duke Orsino to control privateering and piracy. How does Antonio fall short of justifying his attacks on the *Phoenix* and the *Tiger* and his theft of cargo? How does the maiming of Titus justify the Duke's grudge against Antonio?

10. Summarize the importance of wooing to the plot. Why does Duke Orsino put more faith in Cesario's delivery of a message to Olivia than in Valentine's skill? Why does Shakespeare ridicule Sebastian's courtship by a woman?

11. Discuss the centrality of a thought-provoking line: "Some are born great, some achieve greatness, and some have greatness thrown upon them." Which characters are achievers? inheritors? lucky? How does the line illuminate interpretations of Malvolio's egotism?

12. Account for the role of the parasite in ancient and Elizabethan comedy. Why does Olivia tolerate Sir Toby's freeloading, late hours, singing, and alcoholism? How does Sir Toby fool Sir Andrew into paying for late-night drinking sprees?

13. In what ways is Viola a worthy daughter, twin, messenger, consoler, and lover? How does she exhibit compassion for a fellow female trapped in a hopeless relationship? Why does Viola blame men for deceiving vulnerable women?

14. Predict the strengths and weaknesses of the three marriages. Which wife is most likely to demand equality? to feel happily mated? to be truly loved? to make a worthy parent? What strengths may derive from the interrelated couples?

15. Discuss the value of this play as an undercover criticism of Puritanism in the Elizabethan era. Why does Shakespeare typify pious religious fanatics as fraudulant? victimizing? uncompassionate? boring?

16. Make a chart of the value in these details to the comedy:

pearl	yellow hose	candle
dueling	wallet	picture of Olivia
private chapel	bear-baiting	dark room
fake beard	tipping a jester	piracy
sightseeing	spurious ring	eavesdropping
Capilet	Pythagoras	Titus's injury
Dr. Dick	*Phoenix* and *Tiger*	Canary wine
boxwood hedge	veil	the Elephant

Which details express cruelty? teasing? affection? terror? suffering? vengeance? loyalty? crime? social convention? stage convention? milieu?

17. Research the importance of marriage to the aristocratic social order in Shakespeare's day. What does Viola's secret courtship of Duke Orsino imply about the needs of a lone, defenseless girl to negotiate for herself? How does her choice of a husband differ from the Countess Olivia's courtship of Cesario and Sebastian?

18. Explain the theme of illusion versus reality as it applies to these situations:

    - Sir Andrew's challenge letter
    - Antonio's anger about Viola's refusal to lend him money
    - Malvolio's study of his shadow
    - Olivia's belief that she should mourn her brother for seven years
    - the wounding of Sir Toby
    - Feste's pose as the bearded priest Sir Topas
    - Viola's grief for her drowned brother

    How does Sebastian's appearance in Act V precipitate multiple solutions to confusion?

19. Justify the use of love tokens as a means of communication between single males and females. What does the ring mean to Viola? to Olivia? to Malvolio? What does the pearl mean to Sebastian? Why does the picture of Olivia have more value than either the ring or the pearl?

20. Compose an extended definition of displacement using as models the confusions of the plot. Why do the captain and Antonio befriend outsiders in Illyria? How does Viola's disguise as a eunuch further mix-ups between characters? Why does Maria's letter encourage Malvolio's fantasy about social advancement through marriage?

21. Summarize the tone of the repeated line "For the rain it raineth every day." Why does Shakespeare begin the play with a storm at sea and close with remarks about the persistence of bad weather on humankind? How does the repeated line reflect on the play's full title: *Twelfth Night; or, What You Will*? Why do literary historians refer to the comedy as one of Shakespeare's "problem plays"?

22. Summarize male attitudes toward dueling. What do Sir Toby's lies about fierce swordsmen contribute to the parody of a serious, deadly social convention? Why does honor force men to indulge in violence that could result in one of two deaths or permanent maimings? How does Cesario dishonor himself?

23. Define comic relief with examples from drunken carousing, singing rounds, and plotting pranks against Malvolio and Sir Andrew. Why does Shakespeare add Fabian to the co-conspirators?

24. Justify the marriage of Maria and Sir Toby. What arouses his admiration for her? How does she display more character and creativity than he? Which character is more loyal to the Countess Olivia, Maria or Uncle Toby?

25. How does Shakespeare contrast male and female values? Consider these instances:

    - Duke Orsino's withdrawal to a bower to enjoy a melancholy mood
    - the Countess Olivia's covering of her face with a veil
    - Malvolio's fantasy about three months of marriage to the Countess
    - Sebastian's apology for wounding Olivia's uncle
    - Viola's willingness to die for Orsino
    - Orsino's belief that no woman's love can equal his passion

26. Discuss the boasts of Sir Andrew to 3,000 ducats a year, skill at a stringed instrument and at dancing, training in French, learned conversation, and agility as a swordsman. Why does Duke Orsino make no boasts of money or skill other than passionate love for Olivia?

27. Explain the significance of these absent characters to the plot:

    - drowned passengers
    - Titus
    - Sebastian of Messaline
    - Olivia's brother
    - Olivia's father
    - Pythagoras

28. How does the last scene illustrate human faults of jealousy, rage, retaliation, greed, and deception? Why is Malvolio likely to live up to his name, which means "evil wishes"?

29. Summarize the importance of rescue to the plot. Which characters are most in need of rescue? of solace? of a mate? Why does Sir Toby believe that grief is bad for his niece's health? Why does Maria try to rescue Sir Toby from alcoholism?

30. Explain how Shakespeare uses lowly people in a drama that features a duke, countess, and priest. How do cast members like a pirate, sea captain, messenger, steward, officers, sailors, and servant boy contribute to the action?

31. Summarize Shakespeare's misgivings about Puritan meddlers. How did Puritans inhibit the theater business in Elizabethan London? How did English history prove the playwright correct in suspecting Puritans of creating havoc?

32. Propose reasons why Elizabethan audiences liked plays about troubled courtships, meddling, mischief, revenge, confused identity, matrimony, gender swapping, generosity, foppery, drunkenness, and happy endings. What current performances echo those themes?

33. Characterize the role of the trickster by describing Feste and Maria's power over Malvolio and their willingness to subject him to immurement and to public ridicule.

34. Research standard treatment for the insane in Shakespeare's day. Determine the difference between true lunacy and a "midsummer madness." Why were wealth and social caste factors in the quality of care Malvolio could expect?

35. Why does Shakespeare build sympathy for Viola when she confesses that the mix-ups are "too hard a knot for me t'untie"? How does her vulnerability contrast the behaviors of the Duke? the Countess? Maria? Sir Toby? Malvolio? Sebastian?

36. What does gender ambiguity reveal about Shakespeare's era? Why were politicians determined to find a husband for Queen Elizabeth I? Why did she cling to powermongering while denying herself marriage to the man she loved? How did public tensions about the queen's marital status influence the way that Shakespeare presented the persistent courtship of an unwilling woman?

37. Discuss various forms of power over characters. Include these examples:

    - Sir Toby's influence as the uncle of the Countess Olivia
    - the Countess Olivia's wealth and prestige as a lure to Sebastian
    - Sir Andrew's 3,000 ducats per year
    - Sebastian's skill with a sword against Sir Andrew and Sir Toby
    - Duke Orsino's control of Valentine and Cesario
    - the brother guardianship of his orphaned sister Olivia
    - Feste's witty replies to Olivia's threats of punishment
    - Sir Topas's capacity as consoler to a madman
    - Antonio's influence as rescuer of Sebastian
    - the captain's possession of Viola's secret
    - the Duke's anger at Antonio's piracy
    - Viola's willingness to die a thousand times for the Duke's sake

38. Why does Feste have reason to parody Duke Orsino's emotional instability in the lugubrious love song "Come Away Death"? Why does the jester claim that Orsino's "mind is a very opal"? Why does Orsino wallow in lovesickness?

39. How does Shakespeare's use of a central character dressed as a man and wooed by a woman satirize the all-male theatrical company? What type of actor would relish the role of Viola/Cesario?

40. How does Duke Orsino enhance gender complication by threatening to "sacrifice the lamb that I do love"? Why does Antonio's pursuit of Sebastian suggest male-to-male love?

Notes

Notes

Notes